GW00691517

Bizarre
Fantasy
Cricket
XIs

DAVID KOHN

David Kohn is one of the great might-have-beens of world cricket. As a young batsman he was peerless, scoring mountains of runs and showing no fear ... until his older brother stopped using a tennis ball and started using a hard one.

Unable to develop his leg-side game – the lounge window was on that side – he switched to bowling. He showed pace, guile and penetration, but his progress was stopped abruptly when he was no-balled repeatedly for an allegedly bent arm. Thanks a lot, Dad.

Kohn was never the same afterwards, but managed nevertheless to produce many years of mediocrity for school, college and club. Only recently was he forced to retire despite earnest pleas from his teammates … to give up years earlier.

Now reduced to armchair spectating, he yarns about how good the game was in his day, bemoans current standards of on-field behaviour and clings resolutely to the belief that England might one day be good again. He also spends many futile hours trying to persuade his kids that cricket is interesting, really, and that he should be allowed to watch it on TV rather than *Postman Pat* or *Teletubbies*.

This is David Kohn's third book, following the imaginatively-titled *Bizarre Fantasy Football XI's* and *Bizarre Fantasy Rugby XV's,* which was co-written by Nick Brownlee.

'Sorry, coach, I'm crocked. Do you think David Kohn might agree to take over from me?'

Bizarre Fantasy Cricket XIs

DAVID KOHN

generation

To Dawn – Thanks for letting me indulge my obsession and always being there for me
To Samuel, Anna and Jacob – Please could one of you grow up to take an interest in our glorious game
To John Wisden – I don't know where I'd be without you

GENERATION PUBLICATIONS
Editor Phil McNeill
Design Generation Studio (Paul Sudbury and Chris Young)
Research Mark Crossland
Publications Manager Eve Cossins
Publishers David Crowe and Mark Peacock
Thanks to Joseph Crowe, Catherine Killingworth, Peter Baxter and Phil Tufnell

All photographs courtesy of Allsport
with special thanks to Rob Harborne

First published in Great Britain in 2000 by
Generation Publications
9 Holyrood Street, London SE1 2EL
genpub@btinternet.com
Text copyright © Generation Publications
All rights reserved
CIP data for this title is available from the British Library
ISBN 1 903009 22 7

Production by Mike Powell & Associates (01494 676891)
Reprographics by Media Print (UK) Ltd
Printed and bound in Slovenia by arrangement with Korotan-Ljubljana d.o.o.

OWZAT!!

'Arise, Sir Porkalot!'

Bzzrrppp! 'Ah, that's better!'

FOREWORD BY PHIL TUFNELL

C ricket is a great game for indulging your fantasies – whether it's what you'd like to do to the umpire, what you'd like to do after the game, or even what you'd like to get up to with the girl sunning herself in the third row of the stand.

With all that sitting around for days on end (often with no guarantee of anyone actually winning or losing), the players are always looking for new ways to pass the time. In the Middlesex dressing room, one of our favourites is to select our own Bizarre Fantasy Cricket XIs. For some unknown reason, I usually tend to get picked as the captain of the Ugly Blokes XI – so it was a bit of a result when I opened this book and found myself in the rather cool Mavericks XI.

If you're an England supporter, you probably feel that your sense of humour has been tried to the limit over the past few seasons, in which case I hope this book provides an antidote. At the very least, it might help you while away the minutes between the start and finish of the next England innings.

Cheers!

Tuffers in training for the Middlesexshire Morris Dancing Championships

'Cheer up, son, you'll soon be off for a rest at long on'

Phil 'The Cat' Tufnell in that familiar catlike fielding pose

Phil looked high and low for the beer, but alas in vain

The little master: India's favourite pin-up, superstar Sachin Tendulkar

The
GENIUS
XI

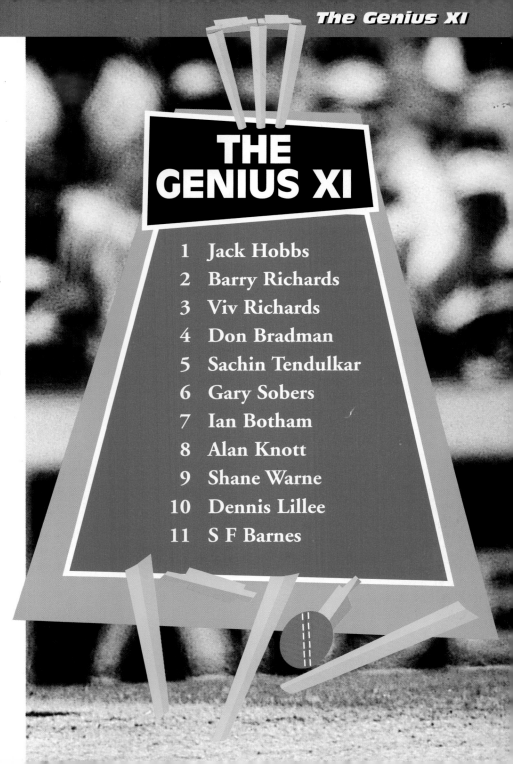

THE GENIUS XI

1 Jack Hobbs
2 Barry Richards
3 Viv Richards
4 Don Bradman
5 Sachin Tendulkar
6 Gary Sobers
7 Ian Botham
8 Alan Knott
9 Shane Warne
10 Dennis Lillee
11 S F Barnes

Cricket is a difficult game to dominate. There are so many variables. You have to cope with the pitch, the weather, the shape of the ball and, most unpredictably of all, the umpires. You have eleven players against you, each with their own distinctive skills. And, as I'm sure we've all felt after getting out for a fourth duck in a row or taking nought for a lot, luck does play a major part.

Rest assured, if you do show signs of being any good, the opposition will try to identify any tiny weakness in your game and relentlessly probe it until they have undermined your technique, confidence and, indeed, your whole reason for being.

The players selected in this XI have risen above this. They have singlehandedly won not only Tests, but Test series. They have struck fear and despair into the hearts of the opposition. They have dominated and they have dominated consistently. So let us begin by paying homage to those players who can be described only as ... The Genius XI.

JACK HOBBS

Jack Hobbs, whose first-class career extended from 1905 to 1934, remains to most informed observers the finest opening bat the world has ever seen. The statistics speak volumes – over 61,000 runs – a record that stands to this day and will never be bettered; 197 centuries – likewise; a career average of 50.65 and an even higher Test average of 56.95; the first man to score 5,000 runs in Tests and the first cricketer to be knighted. But the statistics do not tell the whole story.

Hobbs' technique was flawless – partly as a result of learning to play with a cricket stump as a bat – and he could play on all sorts of wickets against all varieties of bowling. He got better as he got older, scoring 3,000 runs in a season aged 42, averaging 82 in a season aged 45 and opening the batting for England aged 47. He would surely have scored more had he not given his wicket away on many occasions in order to give other batsmen a chance!

He remained modest and a true gentleman, and contemporaries, both teammates and opponents alike, judged him to be an all-time great.

> *"It were 'ard work bowlin' at 'im, but it were something you wouldn't 'ave missed for nothing."*
> – *A FAST BOWLER OF THE TIME*

BARRY RICHARDS

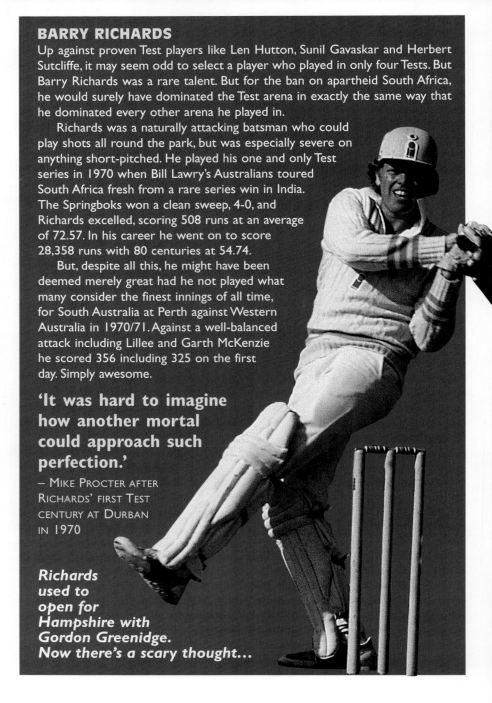

Up against proven Test players like Len Hutton, Sunil Gavaskar and Herbert Sutcliffe, it may seem odd to select a player who played in only four Tests. But Barry Richards was a rare talent. But for the ban on apartheid South Africa, he would surely have dominated the Test arena in exactly the same way that he dominated every other arena he played in.

Richards was a naturally attacking batsman who could play shots all round the park, but was especially severe on anything short-pitched. He played his one and only Test series in 1970 when Bill Lawry's Australians toured South Africa fresh from a rare series win in India. The Springboks won a clean sweep, 4-0, and Richards excelled, scoring 508 runs at an average of 72.57. In his career he went on to score 28,358 runs with 80 centuries at 54.74.

But, despite all this, he might have been deemed merely great had he not played what many consider the finest innings of all time, for South Australia at Perth against Western Australia in 1970/71. Against a well-balanced attack including Lillee and Garth McKenzie he scored 356 including 325 on the first day. Simply awesome.

'It was hard to imagine how another mortal could approach such perfection.'
– MIKE PROCTER AFTER RICHARDS' FIRST TEST CENTURY AT DURBAN IN 1970

Richards used to open for Hampshire with Gordon Greenidge. Now there's a scary thought...

VIV RICHARDS

Hard to credit, but Isaac Vivian Alexander Richards failed on his Test debut. Aged 22, playing against India at Bangalore in 1974, he scored 4 in the first innings and 3 in the second. It was a rare setback. He came back to score 192 not out in his second Test and never looked back.

His dominance was born out of three great attributes – fantastic eyesight and an ability to pick the ball very early; great physical strength and speed; and that indefinable asset, presence. He could impose himself on the opposition at will and undermine what self-confidence they had. He was particularly severe on England. In 1976 – a year in which he scored a record 1,710 Test runs – he scored two double hundreds and averaged 118 for the series. In the 1979 World Cup Final he scored 138 not out including a six over deep square off the last ball – an off-stump yorker! In 1984 at Old Trafford he scored 189 not out – then the highest score in a one-day international; and most imperiously of all, his 110 in 58 balls at Antigua in 1985/6.

From 1976 to 1988, when Richards was at his peak, England's record against West Indies read played 29, lost 20, won NIL! A man whom all English fan hated to love, Viv Richards truly was a giant.

BALL BY BALL Richards' fastest Test hundred	
..36126141	(24 off 10 balls)
.211.412.1	(36 off 20 balls)
112.2111..	(45 off 30 balls)
.1.1624441	(68 off 40 balls)
12..664612	(96 off 50 balls)
..21.461	(110* off 58 balls)

Against England (who else?) in 1986

"He had the best eye of any cricketer I ever saw – and felt that any moment of any match that he was not batting was wasted." – IAN BOTHAM

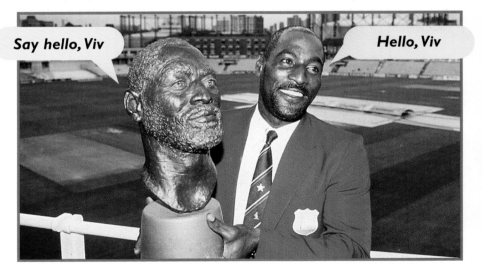

Say hello, Viv

Hello, Viv

SACHIN TENDULKAR

Sachin Tendulkar has been around so long, it's hard to believe he is still only in his mid-20s. Having played his first Test at 16 and scored five Test centuries before his 20th birthday, he has deservedly become cricket-mad India's biggest superstar.

The most technically correct of current Test batsmen, he never seems to play a false shot. Although he can sometimes be vulnerable to an outswinger early in his innings, he is beautifully balanced and his off drive is textbook. His footwork is fast and precise and, like Gavaskar before him, his defence is impeccable.

But he is no automaton – indeed, he has hit more one-day hundreds than any other player. Tendulkar is the outstanding Test batsman of his generation, and for that earns his place in this line-up.

"He plays very much the same as I played … the compactness, his stroke production and technique." – DON BRADMAN

"He is sent from upstairs to play." – RAVI SHASTRI ON 15-YEAR-OLD TENDULKAR

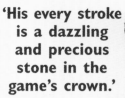

'His every stroke is a dazzling and precious stone in the game's crown.'
– NEVILLE CARDUS 1930

The greatest player of his generation...

DON BRADMAN

The first name on any fantasy XI teamsheet would have to be 'The Don', the dominant batsman of his and any other generation. His statistics are legendary: for want of four more runs in his final Test innings he would have had a Test average of 100. His career average in all first-class matches was 95.14. He hit a century every *three* innings. He was never satisfied with simply scoring a hundred – he passed 300 *six* times. He was, in a word, unstoppable.

Born in a remote part of New South Wales, Australia, Bradman was never coached 'properly'. As a result he was able to give full rein to his innate gifts. He had quick feet, a good eye and, like all great batsmen, made his strokes very late. All the shots were at his command.

In such a career it is difficult to pick out highlights. He was probably at his peak in the 1930 series in England, when he scored 974 runs in the Tests at 139.1. In his first innings on the tour he scored 236 at Worcester, followed by 185 not out at Leicester. In his next innings he made 78 on a soft wicket vs Yorkshire. The subsequent newspaper headline "Bradman fails" says it all.

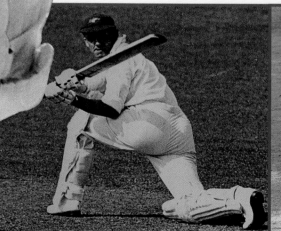

Right: His last innings. Greeted with three cheers by England, Bradman (on left in pic) was out for a duck, so his career average fell 0.06 short of 100

...shame that he had to be a bloody Aussie!

SHANE WARNE

Nothing prepared the world of cricket for the arrival of Shane Warne in the early 1990s. Overweight and sporting an earring and a peroxide blond hairstyle, he looked anything but a first-class cricketer. How appearances can deceive.

He announced himself in England with 'that ball', a delivery to Mike Gatting that constitutes one of the most dramatic moments in cricket history. The ball pitched outside leg and Gatting, a fine player of spin, thrust out a pad to protect his leg stump. He, and everyone watching, with the exception of Warne, was stunned to see the ball turn square and hit his off stump.

Shane Warne has continued to produce extraordinary feats and has consistently won Test matches for Australia. Even when not taking wickets, his control is such that he can tie up an end for a session. He claims to be able to produce five different deliveries, including two that as yet have no name. With a record like his, would any batsman care to argue?

> 'The remarkable thing is he lands the ball on the spot every time. He is the best of his type I have ever seen.'
>
> – RICHIE BENAUD

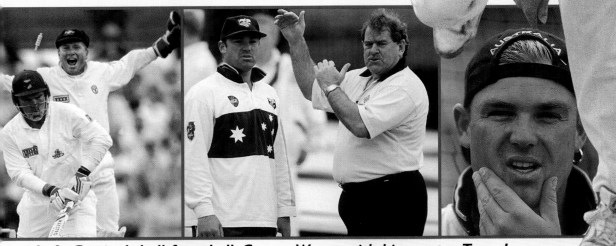

Left: Gatting's ball from hell. Centre: Warne with his mentor, Terry Jenner, who is seen demonstrating the spinner's art of eating two Big Macs at once

'Give us a top-up and I'll show you my middle stump...'

'The greatest matchwinner the game has ever known.'
— MIKE BREARLEY

IAN BOTHAM

For any England fan of the last 25 years, schooled on mediocre player after mediocre player wearing the three lions, one cricketer stands out as world-class. Ian Botham was the British Sobers, a man who could bowl, bat, catch and single-handedly win Test matches.

His achievements are many. Five wickets (including Greg Chappell as his first victim) in his first Test innings; most wickets for England; most catches for England; a century and 'five-for' in the same Test a record five times; most sixes in a season; 14 Test hundreds. Forget the crap haircut and failed attempt on Hollywood, this man was the genuine article.

Few will need reminding of his amazing performances in 1981 against Australia. After a pair at Lord's he 'gave up' the captaincy and very nearly his place in the side. He came back to score 50 and 149 at Headingley to take England to the most improbable win in their history. He took 5 for 1 in 26 balls at Edgbaston to give England another unlikely win. Then at Old Trafford he hit what he felt was his best innings – 118 from 102 balls including six sixes – to secure the series. All who witnessed it will never forget it.

ALAN KNOTT

Alan Knott was a permanent fixture in the England cricket team from his debut in 1967 right up to his defection to Kerry Packer in 1977. He played 95 times in total for his country, and in his first-class career took 1,211 catches and made 133 stumpings. He also scored over 18,000 first-class runs.

As a keeper his technique was not always conventional, but it was faultless. He developed his own natural style, and was unconcerned how he looked or whether he was following the textbook.

The same was true of his batting, which was original and unpredictable. He developed different methods to deal with fast bowling and spinners, but was equally effective against both. In his Test career he averaged 32.75 – high for a keeper – and scored five hundreds.

Knott practised assiduously and kept himself fit throughout his career, enabling him to play for 22 seasons. England have never really replaced him.

"A more or less automatic selection for any team on the basis of his 'keeping alone, he was also a genius – a minor genius – with the bat."
— MIKE BREARLEY

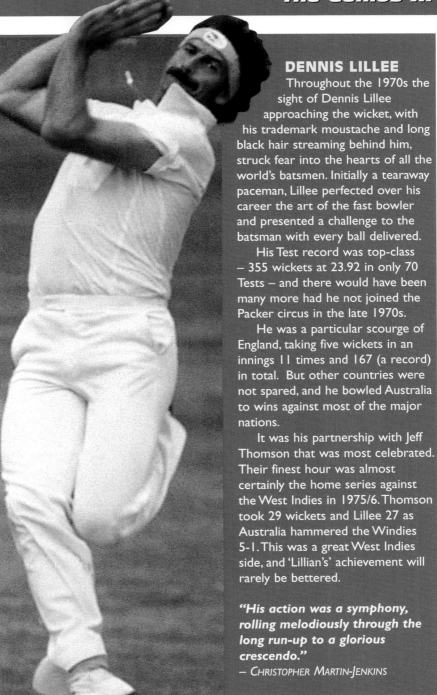

DENNIS LILLEE

Throughout the 1970s the sight of Dennis Lillee approaching the wicket, with his trademark moustache and long black hair streaming behind him, struck fear into the hearts of all the world's batsmen. Initially a tearaway paceman, Lillee perfected over his career the art of the fast bowler and presented a challenge to the batsman with every ball delivered.

His Test record was top-class – 355 wickets at 23.92 in only 70 Tests – and there would have been many more had he not joined the Packer circus in the late 1970s.

He was a particular scourge of England, taking five wickets in an innings 11 times and 167 (a record) in total. But other countries were not spared, and he bowled Australia to wins against most of the major nations.

It was his partnership with Jeff Thomson that was most celebrated. Their finest hour was almost certainly the home series against the West Indies in 1975/6. Thomson took 29 wickets and Lillee 27 as Australia hammered the Windies 5-1. This was a great West Indies side, and 'Lillian's' achievement will rarely be bettered.

"His action was a symphony, rolling melodiously through the long run-up to a glorious crescendo."
— CHRISTOPHER MARTIN-JENKINS

'In all but forty years of watching cricket I rate Gary Sobers as the greatest of all-rounders who have graced the scene in my time.'

E W SWANTON, 1966

GARY SOBERS

As a player Gary Sobers had everything. He could bowl – in three different styles; he could field; he could catch; and, boy, could he bat. On his retirement from Test cricket he held the record for aggregate runs – 8,032 at 57.78 – and for a single innings – 365 not out against Pakistan. He had also taken 235 wickets and 109 catches. And, of course, for Nottinghamshire he had become the first batsman to hit six sixes in one over.

Everything Sobers did was marked by a natural grace. Like a cat, he could look relaxed and uninterested when the action was off, but as soon as the ball was bowled or hit there was no one more alert or quick-minded. Neither a front- or a back-foot batter, he played as conditions demanded. To the well-pitched ball, his footwork was decisive and his driving classical. To the shorter ball, he would go back and wait right to the very last before playing his shot. His fantastic reactions and whippy wrists meant he could improvise runs at will.

Knighted in 1974, Sir Garfield Sobers was and remains a legend.

Sobers the bowler (left) finally meets his match in Sobers the batsman

S. F. BARNES

Sydney Francis Barnes could do everything with the ball – inswing, outswing, the off break and, most potently of all, the inswinging leg break.

He played in Tests only against South Africa and Australia, yet managed a strike rate – one wicket every 42 balls – and an average – 16.43 – unequalled by any 20th-century bowler. In 1913 against South Africa he took the most wickets ever in a Test series (49 despite missing the fifth Test) and recorded the then best figures in a match: 17 for 159.

Remarkably, Barnes played only two full seasons of county cricket, preferring instead to play as a club professional and for Minor County Staffordshire. At this level his record was phenomenal – 10 wickets in an innings 12 times, one game in which he took 14 wickets for 13 runs, overall over 5,500 wickets at an average of just over 7.

He played on into his sixties and remained formidable right up to the end. No wonder that cricketers and students of the game from the time in which he played were unanimous in the view that S. F. Barnes was the bowler of the century.

● *When Bradman suggested that W J O'Reilly was the better bowler as he could do all that Barnes did plus bowl the googly, Barnes' reply was: "It's quite true. I never bowled the googly. I never needed it."*

Chris Broad in the days when playing the Aussies wasn't so tough

The
BRIEFLY TOUCHED BY GENIUS
XI

All of us have at some point in our lives woken up after having played a match-winning innings against the world's finest bowlers or taken five for 24 to win the B&H Cup Final.

Sadly, the very act of waking up brings with it the realisation that it was all a dream, while the hard truth is that the closest we are ever likely to get to being seen in cup final at Lord's is if we perform a streak for the TV cameras.

Most of the players featured in this XI must have felt the same. Resoundingly average throughout the majority of their careers, they all achieved instances or periods when nothing could go wrong.

They defied their naturally modest abilities to achieve wondrous things.

Few of them did it whilst wearing an England sweater – more often than not the opposite seemed to apply – but we salute these part-time heroes nevertheless.

THE BRIEFLY TOUCHED BY GENIUS XI

1 Chris Broad
2 A G Ganteaume
3 Allan Border
4 Ireland
5 Kevan James
6 Collis King
7 Alan Smith
8 Bob Massie
9 Nuwan Zoysa
10 Devon Malcolm
11 Ted Alletson

CHRIS BROAD

Chris Broad was not a bad opening bat, indeed he was good enough to play 25 times for England from 1984 to 1989 and average nearly 40. But nothing he did before or since matched up to his 1986/7 tour to Australia. After England had won the First Test, Broad came into his own to score 162 in the Second Test, topped up by hundreds in the next two. He even found time to top-score in two B&H Challenge matches. He was International Player of the Season, and England recorded their last series win (ever?) vs the old foe. Sadly, his purple patch did not last long: Broad played his last Test just two years later in 1989.

KEVAN JAMES

Kevan James has been playing county cricket since 1980, first with Middlesex and since 1985 for Hampshire. He has scored a few runs and taken a few wickets, but throughout that time has never been looked upon as more than a decent county professional.

All this changed in 1996 when the touring Indians came to Southampton. India were cruising at 207 for one when James came on to bowl his 17th over. Four balls later and Rathore, Tendulkar, Dravid and Manjrekar – all Test players – were back in the pavilion.

When Hampshire batted, James scored 103, making him the only person ever to score a ton and take four wickets in four balls in the same match.

After tonking the Aussies, Chris retired to become David Gower's butler

A.G.GANTEAUME

Not much is known about A. G. Ganteaume, but he possesses a record that is unlikely to be repeated at any time in the future – a hundred in his ONLY innings in Test cricket. Pressed into service because of an injury to regular West Indies opener Jeff Stollmeyer, Ganteaume, a 27-year-old clerk in the Trinidad Civil Service, came out to face England at Port of Spain in February 1948. One might have thought his 112 would have been enough to secure another Test. But not for Ganteaume, who did not even get to bat in the second innings.

Perhaps his knock had been felt to be a little slow. Whatever the reasons, he never played for the Windies again – unlike his fellow debutant, a certain Frank Worrell.

IRELAND

In 1969 the West Indian tourists were not yet the force they became in the mid-1970s, but they nevertheless travelled to Londonderry in July in the sure knowledge that they would register an easy win before returning to the mainland. How wrong they were.

Inspired by bowlers O'Riordan – four wickets for 18 runs – and Goodwin – five for 6 – the home team made a mockery of a Windies line-up that included the legendary Clive Lloyd as well as Clyde Walcott, Basil Butcher and, in all, six of the team who had just fought out a Test draw at Lord's.

That the visitors reached 25 was due only to a last-wicket stand of 13 between Shillingford and Blair. Ireland – who knocked off the runs for the loss of one wicket – had to wait 28 years for their next giant-killing escapade. West Indies, as we all know, became almost unbeatable.

WINDIES' WORST NIGHTMARE
HOW THE MIGHTY FELL

Camacho	1	(1 for 1)
Carew	0	(1 for 2)
Foster	2	(3 for 3)
Butcher	2	(6 for 4)
Lloyd	1	(6 for 5)
Shepherd	0	(12 for 6)
Findlay	0	(12 for 7)
Walcott	6	(12 for 8)
Roberts	0	(12 for 9)
Blair	3	(25 all out)
Shillingford	9*	

Allan Border proves that even Aussie batsmen can bowl better than England

COLLIS KING

Collis King was a hard-hitting middle-order batsman who, despite playing nine times for West Indies between 1976 and 1980, never made it to the top table in Test cricket.

But his finest hour came in the 1979 World Cup Final against England. King arrived at the wicket with his team on the rack at 99 for four. He immediately took a fancy to the short Tavern boundary and to the part-time bowling of Messrs Boycott, Larkins and Gooch. He raced to 86 off 66 balls and dominated a stand of 139 with no less a man than the in-prime-form Viv Richards. West Indies went on to win comfortably, and Collis King went on to do not very much.

ALLAN BORDER

Allan Border was a rather successful cricketer. He holds the record for most Tests played, most runs scored, most Tests as captain and most catches. In a career of such distinction, what could he possibly have done to justify his selection for this XI?

It came on the West Indies tour to Australia in 1988/9. The Windies had won the first three Tests and came to Sydney for the Fourth Test confident of moving towards a 'blackwash'. Australia, not for the first time at Sydney, had prepared a real 'bunsen' and selected two spinners, Peter Taylor and Trevor Hohns. Little did they know that their hero would be Border, who took seven for 46 and four for 50 to lead the green and gold to a seven-wicket win. As he took only 28 wickets in his other 155 Test matches, this could justifiably be seen as being briefly touched by genius.

DEVON MALCOLM

Much as we all loved him for his bottletop glasses and inept fielding, and took his side in his battles with Ray Illingworth, most of us would have to admit that as a Test bowler Devon Malcolm (or Malcolm Devon if you're Ted Dexter) was distinctly ordinary. Yes, he was fast, but the radar was out of order so often that any decent haul of wickets was considered a bonus rather than a right.

Until, that is, Fanie de Villiers of South Africa made the mistake of bouncing him at The Oval in 1994. The ball hit Devon square on the helmet and the normally placid fast bowler was heard to growl: "You guys are history."

He came steaming in for the Springboks' second innings and reduced them to 1 for 3. Only Daryl Cullinan stood firm as Devon took the first seven wickets. Gough rather ruined the show by claiming Cullinan, but Malcolm still finished with 9-57, the best analysis since Laker. Malcolm never did the same again, but should be remembered forever for his brief flash of genius.

Malcolm's big day – another selectorial hit for Dexter Ted

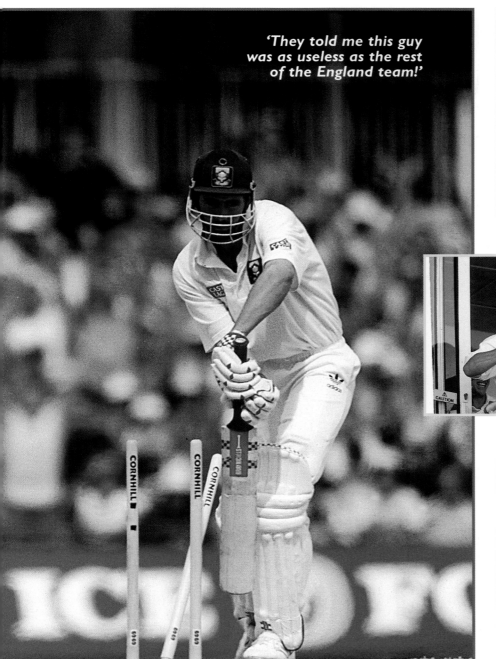

'They told me this guy was as useless as the rest of the England team!'

The England players, like the rest of cricket, can't believe it

'Hang on, lads, I've never had to open one of these before'

Two men with a lot in common – neither lasted long at No.10

23

BOB MASSIE

In the past three decades we've become used to seeing England capitulate abysmally when playing at the home of cricket. 1972 was no different. The visiting Australians had lost the First Test but brought in two debutants, Ross Edwards and Bob Massie, for the match at Lord's. No one could have anticipated the impact that Massie would make.

The conditions favoured swing, and swing was Massie's forte. With Dennis Lillee operating with great pace and hostility from the other end, he had the ideal foil. And he bowled with superb length and accuracy, achieving late swing both ways. The results were dramatic – 8 for 84 in the first innings and 8 for 53 in the second; a match total of 16 for 137.

Massie never quite scaled those heights again, and played only five more Tests. His sideburns went on to be worn with distinction by Malcolm Macdonald but Massie himself faded into relative obscurity. Nothing, however, can dim the memory of five fantastic days in 1972.

A. C. SMITH

Alan Smith was wicketkeeper captain of Warwickshire when they arrived in Clacton to play Essex in 1965. Warwicks had lost two front-line bowlers to the Test side, and lost another, Webster, by the time they came to bowl at the Essex second innings.

Smith, having taken a princely total of 24 wickets in the previous seven seasons, did what any self-respecting captain would do. Handing over the pads and gloves to team-mate Dennis Amiss, he came on first change.

Six overs later, Smith was sitting on the amazing figures of 6-6-0-4. He had shot out both the Essex openers plus Keith Fletcher and Trevor Bailey. It was all too good to last, and Essex managed to bat out for the draw, but Smith's spell must be the best ever by a 'keeper.

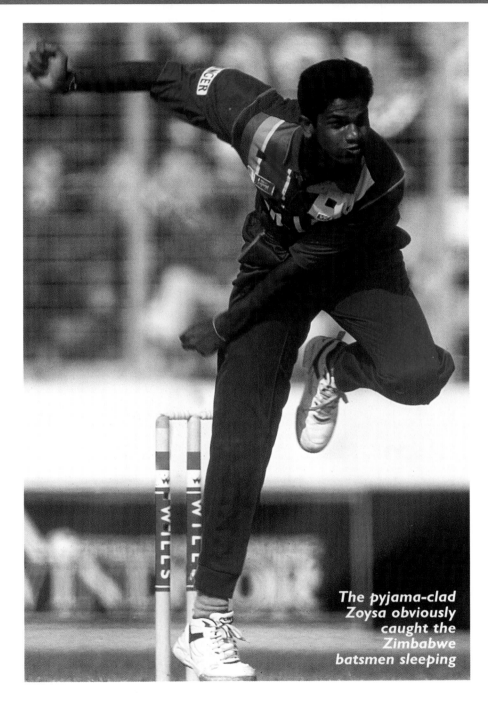

The pyjama-clad Zoysa obviously caught the Zimbabwe batsmen sleeping

NUWAN ZOYSA

Even this early in his career, Nuwan Zoysa would admit that he is unlikely to repeat his astonishing start for Sri Lanka against Zimbabwe in November 1999.

Coming on to bowl the second over with the score still on nought, Zoysa got straight down to business. After one ball the score was nought for one; after two it was nought for two; after three, nought for three. A hat-trick in his first three balls and Gripper, Goodwin and Johnson all back in the pavilion! As for Zoysa, he took only one more wicket in the series.

TED ALLETSON

Tales of high-scoring lower-order batters abound, but none has quite the violence of Ted Alletson's knock against Sussex in 1911. Alletson, who was only in the side because of injury, arrived at the wicket in the second innings with Notts seven wickets down and only nine runs ahead. He began sensibly. By lunch he had scored 47 and Notts had pushed their lead to 84 but with only one wicket left.

Whether the captain told him over the pork chop to hit out or whether a screw simply loosened itself in Alletson's head is unknown. What is known is that Alletson launched a frightening assault on the Sussex bowling. He scored 142 off 51 balls including eight sixes and 18 fours. Notts gained a draw, and Alletson's century was the only one of his career.

ALLETSON'S 51 BALLS

```
0 4 4 1 2 4 2 0 1 6 0 4 2
4 6 4 0 6 3 4 4 0 2 1 4 6
0 4 3 4 6 6 0 4 4 4 6 0 0
0 0 4 4 2 2 6 1 4 4 0 W
```

Five Classic CONFRONTATIONS

In cricket, nobody enjoys an easy victory. There is simply no satisfaction to be gained from beating an opposition who have neither the talent nor appetite to compete. The only true fulfilment is to be found in encountering your equals, fighting a good fight and then coming out on top. In England's case this includes beating the United Arab Emirates and Holland – but, hey, beggars can't be choosers. For this section we select five of the best head-to-heads from cricket folklore. Five of the battles that had us all on the edge of our seats, siding with good against evil, playing every ball for our protagonist. Five classic cricketing confrontations.

BRIAN CLOSE & JOHN EDRICH vs WEST INDIES
OLD TRAFFORD 1976

In 1976 the West Indies began in earnest their campaign to become undisputed heavyweight champions of world cricket. They came, however, to Old Trafford for the Third Test against England with the series still tied at 0-0.

After struggling in their first innings, they skittled England for 71 then piled on the runs to leave England chasing a mere 552 to win. All England had to do was bat out 80 minutes at the end of the third day and then keep going on a cracked, unpredictable pitch for two more days. Oh, and they had to do this against a bowling line-up of Andy Roberts, Wayne Daniel and Michael Holding.

England's openers were the unlikely duo of John Edrich – aged 39 – and Brian Close – aged 45 and playing his first series in nine years. Both had been good players, but their best days were most definitely behind them.

What followed was one of the most brutal displays of short-pitched bowling ever seen. While Edrich attempted to dodge out of the way, Close's main form of defence was to stay put and let the balls thud into his unprotected body. Amazingly, the two stood firm until close of play – when they retired, battered and severely bruised, to the changing room. All was silence as stunned team-mates gaped at Close's weals and wounds. Edrich, sitting head down in a corner suddenly, inexplicably, started laughing uncontrollably. "All that time out there, Closey, and you've only bloody scored one."

Their resistance was to no avail, as England crumbled on the fourth day to leave West Indies handsome victors. And neither Edrich nor Close ever played Test cricket again. But no one who saw it will ever forget their heroic defiance on July 10, 1976.

Close heads another ball to safety

BRIAN LARA vs AUSTRALIA
1999 SERIES

By the time the Aussies made their way to West Indies for the 1999 series, most of the non-Australian cricketing world was profoundly fed up with them. Their claim to be the world's number one was becoming boring. What made it worse was that it was true.

Only one man stood between Australia and another series win: Brian Lara. Since his high summer of 1994, Lara had blown hot and cold and his captaincy had attracted much negative comment on the disastrous tour of South Africa. He desperately needed a good performance.

The start was not propitious. In the First Test, West Indies capitulated to a humiliating total of only 51 in their second innings to lose by 312 runs. Lara's hold on the captaincy hung by a thread.

He responded in the way that only true champions can. He scored 213 in the Second Test as the Windies squared the series with a 10-wicket win, and then scored 153 not out to lead his team to a most dramatic one-wicket win in Bridgetown in the Third.

His 100 in the Fourth Test was not enough to save his team from defeat, but he had proved his point against the strongest, most determined bowling line-up in the world.

Lara can't hide his delight as the Aussies finally lose a game

*David Steele
adds four
pork chops
to his packed
fridge freezer*

DAVID STEELE VS DENNIS LILLEE AND JEFF THOMSON
1975 ASHES SERIES

David Steele remains to this day one of the most unlikely heroes in the history of English cricket.

Steele had been around the county scene for some years when he received a surprise call-up for England at the age of 33 in 1975. England had been battered in the First Test by the Australian bowling line-up of Lillee, Thomson and Max Walker, and needed someone with guts, bravery and determination.

Steele was that man.

Never the greatest stylist or shot-maker, Steele set out with one primary objective. To stay in.

He stuck to his task like a limpet and simply would not allow himself to fail. A 50 in his debut innings was followed up by scores of 45, 73, 92, 39 and 66. His duels with Lillee and Thomson made for gripping TV drama.

He became a national hero on the basis of his deeds and (partly a measure of cricket's popularity at the time) was voted the BBC Sports Personality of the Year.

The Man of Steele also won a vast quantity of lamb chops from a Northamptonshire butcher who offered him one for every run. He's probably still got some now.

'Who the hell is this guy? Groucho Marx?'
JEFF THOMSON TO HIS TEAM-MATES AS DAVID STEELE FIRST ARRIVED AT THE CREASE

SALIM MALIK VS SHANE WARNE
PAKISTAN vs AUSTRALIA
1994/5 AND 1995/6

When Australia toured Pakistan in 1994, two of the world's most competitive and irascible cricket sides were brought together. The central duel in the series was between Australia's best bowler – Shane Warne, who took 18 wickets in the three Tests – and Pakistan's best batsman – captain Salim Malik.

Malik, who claimed to have worked out how to play Warne, batted an incredible 21 hours in the series, amassing a record 557 runs at 92.83.

If Malik thought he had done enough to retain the captaincy for another series, he was wrong. When the Aussies got home, Warne plus Tim May and Mark Waugh accused Malik of trying to bribe them to throw a Test. Malik lost his job and much acrimony followed. This was perhaps a little unfortunate, as Pakistan were visiting Australia later that year.

Fate decreed that Malik and Warne would face each other in the First Test at Brisbane. Unfortunately, Malik injured himself fielding and did not bat until No. 8 in the Pakistan second innings. Warne was bowling. Four balls into his innings Malik played a hesitant leading edge to a top-spinner and was caught.

Malik defiantly returned for the Third Test, scoring 36 and 45 in Pakistan's only win of the three-match series – and this time Warne failed to get his man in the final head-to-head between two fiery rivals.

Left: Salim Malik and his good friend Shane Warne during the 1995/6 series in Australia

29

That's just what you said in Johannesburg in '96, old chap

ALLAN DONALD vs MICHAEL ATHERTON
TRENT BRIDGE 1998

When the South African tourists began bowling at England's second innings in the Fourth Test at Trent Bridge in 1998, they were even more fired up than usual. One-nil up after the Second Test, they had been denied victory in the Third only by freak good batting from Robert Croft, Darren Gough and Angus Fraser. Now it looked as though they might lose the Fourth, having collapsed to 208 in their second innings, leaving England a very makeable 247 to win. Never mind that this was more than England had scored to win a home Test since 1902. South Africa simply had to bowl England out.

Up against them was Michael Atherton, nemesis of the Springboks in 1996 and England's most reliable batsman. Together with Mark Butcher and then Nasser Hussain, Atherton saw off the new ball and took England to 82 for one. Cronje, the South African captain, desperate for a breakthrough, turned to Allan Donald.

Almost immediately, Atherton appeared to glove the umpteenth short ball he had faced to Boucher behind the stumps. The South African celebrations were loud but short-lived as Atherton stood his ground and umpire Steve Dunne ignored the appeal.

For the next 90 minutes, Donald unleashed a furious torrent of fast, aggressive bowling and verbal abuse that had everyone in the ground flinching – except Atherton. Somehow he survived and went on the next day to lead England to a famous win.

31

David lets the dressing room know how big he wants his shepherd's pie

The PORKERS XI

The game of cricket has always been synonymous with eating and drinking. In no other sport do participants break formally for lunch, tea and drinks, and in no other sport would a typical mid-game snack comprise chicken, chips and two veg washed down by jam roly-poly and custard.

Certainly, you would have to go a long way to find a sport in which fairy cakes are considered an integral part of a balanced diet. It is, therefore, no surprise that many cricketers have been of rotund aspect.

In recent years, the demands of the one-day game have meant a greater need for speed. Sadly, this tends to apply to all eleven players on the pitch, even the slips.

As a result, true porkers are fast becoming extinct in the first-class game. So let's raise a large glass to eleven of the finest…

THE PORKERS XI

1 Andy Moles
2 Colin Milburn
3 David Boon
4 Inzamam-ul-Haq
5 Mike Gatting
6 Arjuna Ranatunga
7 Jack Richards
8 Shane Warne
9 Ian Austin
10 Jack Simmons
11 Merv Hughes

Umpire: David Shepherd

Old Merv always was a bit of a fathead…

ANDY MOLES

Andy Moles made a leisurely start to his career, coming into county cricket aged 25 in 1986. This late start did not prevent him from establishing himself quickly as Warwickshire's first-choice opener both on the field and in the canteen. He remained a fixture in the county's first XI for 12 years – they couldn't physically remove him – until he retired in 1998 with both an average and a waist size of over 40.
Fantasy favourite snack:
Warwickshire pork pie

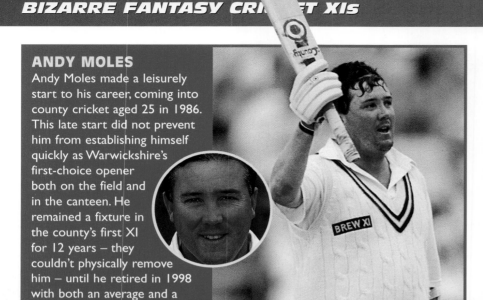

DAVID BOON

David Boon has always said that he owes a lot to another member of this XI – Jack Simmons, who was his first captain and coach at Tasmania. Whether Simmons gave young David dietary as well as cricketing advice is unclear, but Boon has remained, let us say, robust throughout his career. As well as being a superb batsman and a great close-to-the-wicket fielder (good move, Dave) he also holds the record for the largest number of Fosters drunk on an Australia-to-England flight. Respect.
Fantasy favourite snack: Cow pie

COLIN MILBURN

The cruel car accident in May 1969 that deprived Colin Milburn of the sight in his left eye was a tragedy not only for the player himself but for the whole world of cricket. As a player he was just beginning to cement his place in the England line-up with his aggressive, powerful batting. As a man he was full of fun and good cheer. And as for his physique, well he was big. One winter, after a rigorous course of dieting, he weighed in at 16 stone – but he normally hovered closer to the 18 -stone mark. A heavyweight in every sense of the word, his death aged only 48 robbed cricket of one of its true characters.
Fantasy favourite snack: Durham ox

INZAMAM-UL-HAQ

Much of the entertainment in the 1999 Cricket World Cup was provided single-handedly by Pakistan's Inzamam-ul-Haq. His running between the wickets gave us almost enough amusement to make up for England's pathetically early exit from the tournament. Inzamam always appeared to be struggling to propel his bulk from wicket to wicket, and was run out twice as well as almost being lapped by the speedy Moin Khan. Definitely a man who favours a boundary over a quick single.
Fantasy favourite snack: Gulabjam

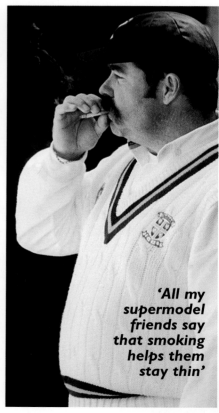

'All my supermodel friends say that smoking helps them stay thin'

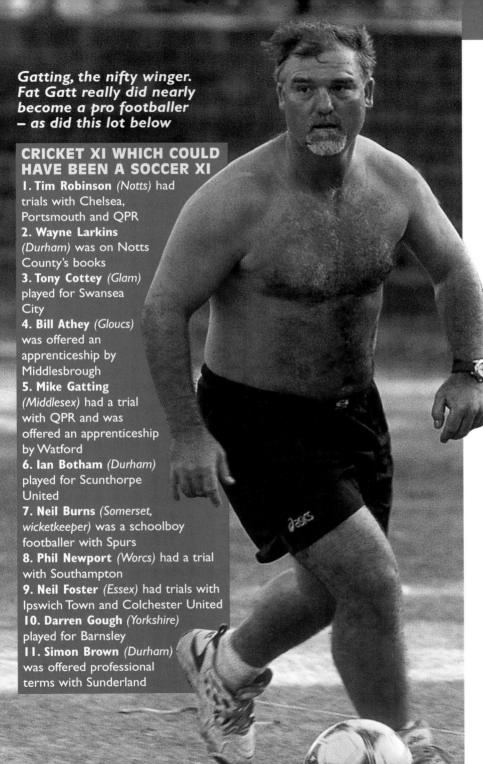

*Gatting, the nifty winger.
Fat Gatt really did nearly
become a pro footballer
– as did this lot below*

CRICKET XI WHICH COULD HAVE BEEN A SOCCER XI

1. Tim Robinson *(Notts)* had trials with Chelsea, Portsmouth and QPR
2. Wayne Larkins *(Durham)* was on Notts County's books
3. Tony Cottey *(Glam)* played for Swansea City
4. Bill Athey *(Gloucs)* was offered an apprenticeship by Middlesbrough
5. Mike Gatting *(Middlesex)* had a trial with QPR and was offered an apprenticeship by Watford
6. Ian Botham *(Durham)* played for Scunthorpe United
7. Neil Burns *(Somerset, wicketkeeper)* was a schoolboy footballer with Spurs
8. Phil Newport *(Worcs)* had a trial with Southampton
9. Neil Foster *(Essex)* had trials with Ipswich Town and Colchester United
10. Darren Gough *(Yorkshire)* played for Barnsley
11. Simon Brown *(Durham)* was offered professional terms with Sunderland

ARJUNA RANATUNGA

An unwritten law in cricket decrees that the captain is allowed to be overweight and unfit. After all, as captain he can field where he likes, he's not going to be surprised by being asked to bowl, and he can do a lot of pointing when the ball speeds past him. Sri Lanka's pocket Napoleon, Arjuna Ranatunga, is probably the least fit player in world cricket, but it doesn't stop him getting around the pitch to be eternally in the batsman's face. Still, any batter knows he could outrun him if things got really nasty.
Fantasy favourite snack:
Sour grapes

MIKE GATTING

Fat Gatt is the icon for cricket's overweight fraternity. Standing 5ft 10in and weighing in at a princely 15st 7lbs, Gatt has clearly gorged a little too frequently at the table of Lord's.

It's hard to believe, but Gatt was once a ballroom dancing champion – apparently they used to have a weebles division – and a triallist for First Division football.

Gatting famously lost his England captaincy over allegations that a barmaid spent time in his room after hours on tour. But as Ian Botham said: "I don't believe it, because I know that nothing goes into Gatt's room after 10.30pm unless he can eat it."
Fantasy favourite snack: *Jam roly poly and custard*

SHANE WARNE

The great bleached whale is clearly a player who needs to watch his weight when out of competition. A frequent target for 'good-natured' abuse from the terraces, Warne is a man of simple culinary tastes. On a diet in India in 1998, he claimed he was "really craving for some canned spaghetti on toast". Ian Healy probably had a more realistic view: "Shane's idea of a balanced diet is a cheeseburger in each hand."

Favourite snack: *Pies (all of them)*

'Go back to the pavilion and deflate yourself, you balloon.'

DARYL CULLINAN OF SOUTH AFRICA AFTER TAKING WARNE'S WICKET

JACK RICHARDS

Overweight 'keepers tend to be a little thin on the ground, so finding one for this team proved a tad difficult. In the end we were able to whittle it down to Geoff Humpage, Ian Gould and Jack Richards – all stalwarts of the late '70s and 1980s. We went for Richards for no good reason other than that he always looked rather gay when keeping.

Fantasy favourite snack: *Sugar puffs*

'Move over, Wayne Sleep...' Lancashire's Ian Austin shows his balletic grace

IAN AUSTIN

Among the more unlikely and pleasant surprises of 1999 was the selection of Ian Austin as one of *Wisden*'s Five Cricketers of the Year. The *Wisden* profile described him as "a burly man", adding that he "still has the air of an old-fashioned pie-and-chips player". He is fit – he certainly claims he is – so in the words of the sage, he either has big bones or … he is lying.

Fantasy favourite snack: *Lancashire hotpot*

Simmons thought about getting one of those aluminium bats as the wooden one struggled to take his weight

MERV HUGHES

When Merv Hughes first burst on to the Test scene he looked suspiciously like a renegade from '80s gay pop icons The Village People. The only giveaway was his beer gut. No gay would ever have a beer gut – it's *soooooh* unattractive! Hughes confided in 1994: "Wickets are more important than waistline." He was right, of course, but did he really have to wear such skin-tight shirts to show off his paunch??

Fantasy favourite food: Tinnies, eaten whole

Right: Merv checks that his tackle is still there, as he hasn't seen it in some time

DAVID SHEPHERD
UMPIRE

During David Shepherd's long first-class playing career, the sight of him heading up the pitch on a quick (well, let's be honest, a rather slow) single was enough to strike fear into any groundsman. "Please, oh please don't run on the wicket – we'll never repair the potholes."

As an umpire he is less likely to interfere with the playing surface, but he remains a large presence. No need for a sightscreen when David's behind the stumps (no need for a heavy roller either). Lovely man. Just don't mention Nelson.

Fantasy favourite food: Anything that doesn't move

JACK SIMMONS

While Ian Austin might "have the air" of a pie-and-chips player, Jack Simmons was the living embodiment of the breed. Flat Jack could never be described as a natural athlete, yet managed to play first-class cricket right up to the age of 48. Simmons eschewed contemporary wisdom on diet and fitness, yet still became a legend in Lancashire and Tasmania. A big man in all senses of the word.

Favourite food: Fish and chips

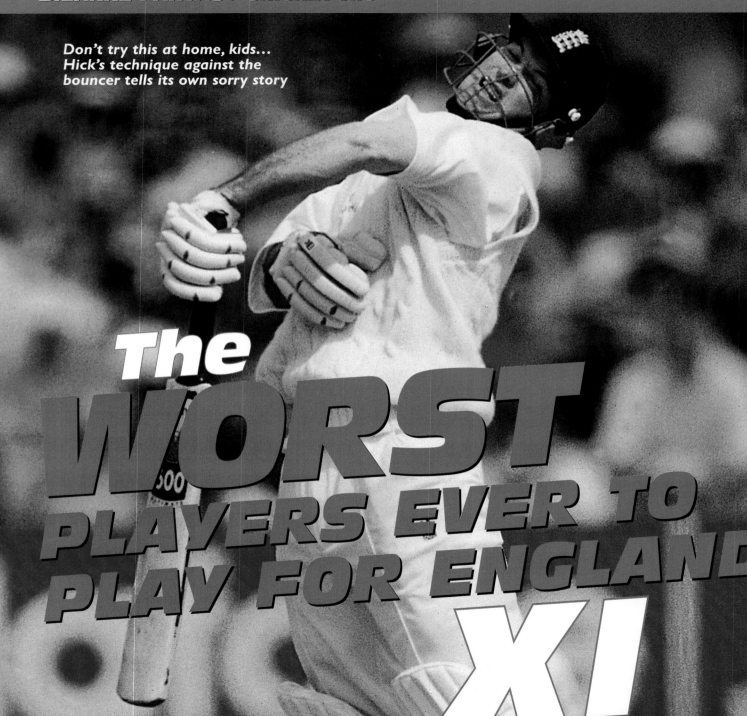

*Don't try this at home, kids...
Hick's technique against the
bouncer tells its own sorry story*

The
WORST
PLAYERS EVER TO
PLAY FOR ENGLAND
XI

See if this sounds familiar. England invents game. Other teams begin to play it. But England are tops! Other teams get the hang of it. They beat England. We spread game to new countries that we can still beat. They learn how to play it. We dive down the world rankings. We try to persuade the governing body to bring in Finland, Iceland, North Korea – anyone – in the vain hope of finding an opponent worse than us.

In cricket, there are numerous reasons why England have sunk so low – no Geoff Boycott for one (I think it was Geoff himself who said that … repeatedly) – not least poor selection. Players who failed to reproduce county form, players who have frozen in the bright lights, players who are simply shite and should never have played cricket in the first place.

So we had an awful lot of players (and a lot of awful players) to choose from for this XI. We have tried to be fair in most cases, but in others have been straightforwardly vindictive. See if you agree with our selection.

THE WORST PLAYERS EVER TO PLAY FOR ENGLAND XI

1. Mark Lathwell
2. Mike Brearley
3. Graeme Hick
4. J. F. Crapp
5. Chris Cowdrey
6. Ben Hollioake
7. Chris Read
8. Tony Pigott
9. Robert Croft
10. Jonathan Agnew
11. Ian Salisbury

MARK LATHWELL

Pundits are always telling us we should have more young players in the national side. "Look at India," they say, "they had an eight-year-old in the team." OK, so he was useless, but it does show a commitment to the future.

What these people fail to remember is that a youth-at-all-costs policy can result in errors of judgment like the selection of 21-year-old Mark Lathwell to open against Australia in 1993. His performance for Somerset against the tourists – 0 and 15 – should have been a clue, but he was still sent in against one of the stronger attacks in world cricket.

As it happens, the lad didn't disgrace himself in his two Tests, but as for the idea of blooding him for the future … well, six years on and he has never been selected to play for England again.

Tests 2, runs 78,
average 19.5

Lathwell's average actually improved when he left his bat behind

Cowdrey's dad was so busy captaining England, he never had time to teach Chris cricket

CHRIS COWDREY
(CAPTAIN)

After Chris Cowdrey toured India in 1984/5, playing five Tests with little distinction, he must have imagined that his England career was over for good. He was wrong.

In 1988, with England 2-0 down against the West Indies and desperate for a new captain, they amazed us all by turning to Cowdrey. "We believe his style of leadership is what is now required," announced the chairman of selectors, Peter May – who also happened to be Cowdrey's godfather.

Chris's captaincy did not get off to the best of starts. The gateman at Headingley did not recognise him and initially refused him entry to the car park. Why couldn't that jobsworth have stuck to his guns?

Tests 6, runs 101, average 14.42; wickets 4, ave 77.25

GRAEME HICK

Has there ever been a more frustrating cricketer than Graeme Hick – over 100 hundreds to his name, more runs than any other current player, a first-class average over 55, a lion in county cricket yet a mouse in the Test arena.

Hick's record in five-day cricket is not that bad compared to many of his England colleagues, but he should have been so much better. He should have been our Lara or Tendulkar … instead he's our Carl Hooper, a perennial under-achiever. It's hard to understand how someone with his record can have so little self-confidence. Now, if only Mike Brearley was his captain…

Tests 54, runs 3,005, average 34.15; wickets 22, average 57.05

JACK CRAPP

Jack Crapp, who played all his Tests in 1948/9, wasn't actually a real stinker. We only selected him out of an infantile desire to make a cheap gag out of his name. That done, we shall move on to the next member of this unillustrious XI.

Tests 7, runs 319, average 29.00

BEN HOLLIOAKE

The wardrobe of English cricket is packed with the skeletons of players labelled "the next Ian Botham". Hollioake is simply the last but one on the production line. He came to prominence for three reasons – some excellent one-day batting performances; having a brother who said he was brilliant (which never worked for me, unfortunately); and being a handsome dog.

Sadly, on the pitch at least, he has failed to live up to his promise. He may come good, but like many a young player before him will have to learn that biffing the ball to all quarters may work in the back garden, but is unlikely to be a tactic for long-term success in Test cricket.

Tests 2, runs 44, average 11.00; wickets 4, average 49.75

Ben Hollioake – oh well, putting an Aussie in the England team seemed a good idea at the time

Cairns' tactic of shouting 'Duck!' as he bowled finally paid off

TONY PIGOTT

A lot of players can consider themselves lucky to have represented their country. But none were luckier than Tony Pigott, the Sussex medium pacer who played his one and only Test in 1983 in New Zealand.

Pigott, who was truly the definition of average, was playing for Wellington when injuries to Neil Foster and Graham Dilley led to his shock call-up for the Second Test. Pigott's joy must have been tempered by the fact that England gave their worst ever Test performance to lose by an innings and 132 runs in a match where New Zealand scored only 307!!

To add insult to injury, Pigott had postponed his wedding to play. Little did he realise that the game would be over in less than three days, which would have given him time to get married, go on honeymoon, and get a quickie divorce as well.

Tests 1, runs 12, average 12; wickets 2, average 37.5

CHRIS READ

It's hard to come up with geniunely poor English wicketkeepers so we've stuck to our theme of putting the boot into England's promising youngsters with this choice. Read was selected against the 'soft' opposition of New Zealand in 1999, as the nation yet again debated the wisdom of playing Alec Stewart as wicketkeeper-batsman. The young man looked capable with the gloves, making eight dismissals on his debut – and he has since shown that he can smite sixes even off Shaun Pollock in the one-day game.

His selection for this XI, however, is based on just one ball. Facing Chris Cairns at Lord's, Read ducked out of the way of what looked to him like a vicious bouncer. Unfortunately, it was Cairns' slower ball, which clean bowled the hapless Read and made him look not a little stupid.

Tests 3, runs 38, average 9.5; dismissals 11 (ct 10/st 1)

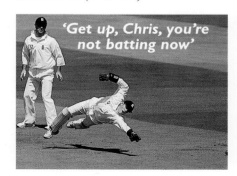

'Get up, Chris, you're not batting now'

ROBERT CROFT

Robert Croft was a bit of a selectors' favourite, largely because he looked like Mike Atherton's brother. Crofty wasn't actually that bad when he started playing for England. However, like many of his compatriots, he seemed to get worse rather than better, the more Tests he played.

As luck would have it, his last home Test provided probably his finest hour – batting for over three hours at Old Trafford to save the Test (and the series) against South Africa in 1998. He was rewarded for this by being dropped for the next game, although this might have had more to do with his not having taken a single wicket in the series.

Tests 15, runs 272, average 15.11; wickets 36, average 38.33

JONATHAN AGNEW

Many younger followers of cricket who know Jonathan Agnew only as 'Aggers' from *Test Match Special* perhaps do not realise that he was once a Test cricketer. A pretty poor one, but a Test cricketer nevertheless.

Aggers was a decent county bowler, good enough to take a hundred wickets in a season and become a *Wisden* Cricketer of the Year in 1988. Perhaps he should have played more Tests than he did. The vagaries of the selectors, however, meant that he played only three and that he departed Test cricket with an average that can be described only as shocking.

Tests 3, runs 10, average 10; wickets 4, average 93.25

'I'm not bowling again unless you promise not to hit it so far'

IAN SALISBURY

Wrist spin is a dying art in England. Sadly, it will continue its demise if the best we can come up with as an example to kids is the hapless Ian Salisbury. The 'English Shane Warne' sadly shares little of his Australian counterpart's gluttonous appetite for wickets. At Test level Salisbury looks about as threatening as a white cloud on a sunny day, and is a master of 'buffet' bowling – come and help yourself. In the absence of anyone better, he will undoubtedly come back to play for England. The batsmen of the world must be shaking … with laughter.

Tests 11, runs 282, average 15.66; wickets 18, average 70

ELEVEN HALF-DECENT PLAYERS WHO NEVER PLAYED FOR ENGLAND

1 **Peter Roebuck** Somerset (*Wisden Cricketer of the Year 1988*)
2 **Darren Bicknell** Surrey
3 **David Byas** Yorkshire
4 **Trevor Jesty** Hants, Surrey & Lancs (*Cricketer of the Year 1983*)
5 **Mark Nicholas** Hampshire
6 **Phil Bainbridge** Gloucestershire & Durham (*Cricketer of the Year 1986*)
7 **Geoff Humpage** Warwickshire (*Cricketer of the Year 1985*)
8 **David Millns** Leicestershire
9 **Peter Hartley** Yorkshire & Hants
10 **Jack Simmons** Lancashire (*Cricketer of the Year 1985*)
11 **Stuart Turner** Essex

As captain, Mike loved to give catching practice ... especially to the opposition

MIKE BREARLEY:
WORST PLAYER...?

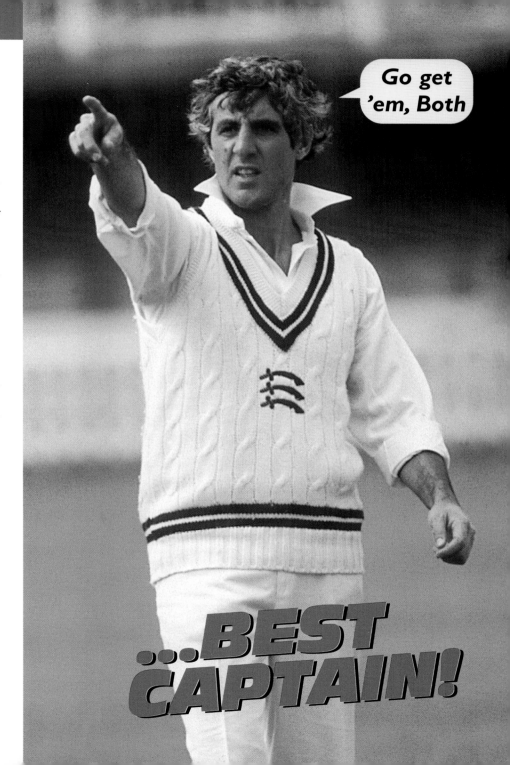

Go get 'em, Both

...BEST CAPTAIN!

MIKE BREARLEY

Michael Brearley is a legend in English cricket. He's the man who brought the best out of Botham, the man who managed to lead England to 18 wins in 31 Tests as captain, the captain who even Boycott had some respect for. He's possibly the most intelligent man to play cricket since the war. Amazingly, people still talk about him coming out of retirement to captain England.

He's also probably the worst opener to play regularly for England in history.

Here are some of the stats: Brearley played 39 Tests for England, scoring 1,442 runs at an average of 22.88. In 66 Test innings he scored *no* centuries. And he had that stupid style with the bat held in mid-air as he waited for the ball.

Sadly, in cricket it is impossible to be a non-playing captain. And, as Ray Illingworth so ably demonstrated, a football-style manager doesn't really work. So to have the best captain, we had to have the worst opener.

Was it worth it? Well, as Botham himself says: "He was quite simply the best captain I have ever played under." We'll take that as a probably then.

'Captaining a side is like teaching at a university – unless you are a genius you will always have students who are better at the subject than you.'

MIKE BREARLEY IN *THE ASHES RETAINED*, HIS BOOK ABOUT THE 1978/9 TOUR OF AUSTRALIA, ON WHICH THE WINNING CAPTAIN'S TEST AVERAGE WAS JUST 16.72

NEW ZEALAND v ENGLAND

Second Test 1984, Christchurch
England travelled to New Zealand in 1984 with a team containing Gower, Gatting, Botham and Lamb and having never before lost a series to the Kiwis. Under the inspirational (well, maybe not) leadership of Bob Willis they arrived in Christchurch for the Second Test, having had marginally the better of the First.

They did not start well. The abysmal England bowling – described by Willis as "some of the worst" he had seen in Tests – allowed the Kiwis to score at 4.2 an over to reach 307. England, requiring only 107 to avoid the follow on, then contrived to be all out for 82. The second innings was little better, with the starry England line-up again failing to reach 100.

Thus, in only 12 hours' play, England managed to be defeated by an innings and 132 runs. If there is a lower point in our history, we don't know it.
New Zealand 307 all out (Hadlee 99); England 82 all out (Chatfield 3-10, Hadlee 3-16, Cairns 3-35); England 93 all out (Hadlee 5-28). New Zealand win by an innings and 132 runs.

Gower is gutted as another defeat means no champagne

ENGLAND'S FIVE WORST TEST DEFEATS

ENGLAND v WEST INDIES

Second Test 1984, Lord's

David Gower. Elegant strokeplayer – yes; good captain – you must be joking. Some would call him unlucky to have had to face the West Indies twice at their peak. Others would simply call him crap.

Gower led England to a 5-0 series whitewash against the Windies in 1984. The bitterest defeat of the five was surely in the Second Test, where England actually declared (albeit with nine wickets down), setting the West Indians a target of 342 to win. What followed was carnage, with Gordon Greenidge playing the innings of his lifetime and Windies scoring at over five an over to cruise to a nine-wicket win. Never has an England bowling attack looked so toothless.

England 286 all out (Fowler 106);
West Indies 245 all out (Botham 8-103);
England 300 for 9 dec (Lamb 110);
West Indies 344 for 1
(Greenidge 214 not out,
Gomes 92 not out).
West Indies win
by nine wickets.

In the end Greenidge batted on his knees to give the England bowlers a chance

ENGLAND v AUSTRALIA

Fifth Test 1989, Trent Bridge

By the time Australia came to Nottingham in 1989, England's series goose was well and truly cooked. Three down with two to play, we were hoping that our opponents' guard would drop and we would gain our usual consolation win. No such luck.

By close of play on the first day the scoreboard read Australia 301 runs scored for *no wickets* conceded. Graham Marsh 125 not out, Mark Taylor 141 not out. And all this despite the debut of the fearsome Malcolm Devon. Australia went on to amass a huge score, we were bowled out twice, another regulation innings defeat was in the bag. Is it dull winning all the time? Ask an Aussie.

Australia 602 for 6 dec (Taylor 219, Marsh 138); England 255 all out (Robin Smith 101, Alderman 5-69); England 167 for 9 (Botham absent). Australia win by an innings and 180 runs.

'It wasn't a great wicket, but Marsh and Taylor stuck it out. England never recovered from that disappointment.'

STEVE WAUGH

47

ENGLAND v AUSTRALIA
Fifth Test 1948, The Oval

The summer of '48 marked the final tour and series for the great Don Bradman. Just short of his 40th birthday, he continued his relentless domination of the English bowlers with two hundreds and an average of over 80 in the first four Tests. He then came to The Oval having already clinched the series 3-0 and looking to provide a final flourish to his glorious career.

Famously, Bradman was out for a duck, bowled by Eric Hollies – but as England had scored only 52 in their first innings, this was not too much of a problem for the green and gold.

If Bradman thought he might have a knock in the second innings and score the four runs he needed to retire with his Test average at 100, well, England had other ideas. They showed some resistance in reaching 153 for three but then lost their remaining seven wickets for 35 (now where have we seen that before?). Australia won by an innings and Bradman had to be satisfied with an average of 99.94.

England 52 all out (Lindwall 6-20);
Australia 389 all out (Morris 196,
Bradman 0);
England 188 all out (Johnston 4-40).
Australia win by an innings and 149 runs.

'It's hard to bat with tears in your eyes.'

DON BRADMAN,
AFTER FALLING TO ERIC HOLLIES
FOR A DUCK IN HIS FINAL
TEST MATCH INNINGS

WEST INDIES v ENGLAND
Third Test 1994, Port-of-Spain

Although we should have long ago given up hope of England ever again being successful, there is a masochistic streak about following the Poms that keeps us coming back for more. We keep thinking, with no basis in reality, that things are going to get better. So it was in Trinidad in 1994 when, after a great effort from Caddick and Lewis (yes, really), we left ourselves with only 194 to

Curtly's first ball: Atherton is already taking his bow. Right: Next, please – Robin Smith is out for a duck

win. Sadly we didn't bank on one of the great bowling spells of all time from Curtly Ambrose. By the time England retired on the fourth day, they had scored 40 for the loss of EIGHT wickets. Ambrose had taken six. Seventeen minutes into the final day we were all out for 46. Well, there's always the next Test...

West Indies 252 all out; England 328 all out (Thorpe 86; Ambrose 5-60);
West Indies 269 all out (Caddick 6-65); England 46 all out (Ambrose 6-24).
West Indies win by 147 runs.

...AND TO CHEER US UP
FIVE BRILLIANT ENGLAND WINS

ENGLAND v AUSTRALIA
Old Trafford 1956
Won by an innings and 170 runs ...
Laker 9-37 in first, 10-53 in second.

ENGLAND v AUSTRALIA
Headingley 1981
Won by 18 runs ... Botham's amazing innings ... Willis 8-43.

AUSTRALIA v ENGLAND
Melbourne 1982/3
Won by 3 runs ... last-wicket drama as Thomson and Border add 70 to take Australia to brink of victory.

WEST INDIES v ENGLAND
Port-of-Spain 1997/8
Won by 3 wickets ... Fraser 9-80 in match ... nail-biting climax to low-scoring game.

ENGLAND v SOUTH AFRICA
Headingley 1998
Won by 23 runs ... series clincher ... certain victory snatched away by Rhodes and Macmillan fight-back ... snatched back by Gough (below).

BIZARRE BATTING LINE-UPS

If you're the sort of person who likes his batsmen trustworthy, solid and reliable in a crisis, then this selection is not for you. We have chosen here a set of batters who would rather score fast than score lots, whose idea of playing themselves in means swinging their bat on the way out to the middle – and who would rather die than defend.

GILBERT JESSOP

Gilbert Jessop, who played from 1894 to 1914, was the prototype for the modern one-day cricketer. He was the most aggressive batsman of his day, could bowl fast and was a phenomenal fielder.

A brilliant all-round sportsman, he was capable of murdering the opposition bowling and frequently outscored his teammates by four or five to one. Never one to protect his wicket, he scored only one century for England. It was, needless to say, the fastest ever by an Englishman.

Finest moment: 157 out of 201 in an hour for Gloucs vs West Indies in 1901

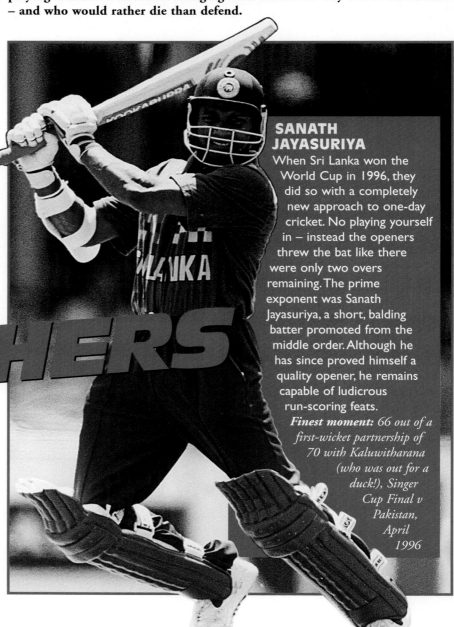

The DASHERS

'No one has ever driven the ball so hard, so high and so often in so many different directions.'

– C. B. FRY ON GILBERT JESSOP

Right: Jaya was ordered to hit boundaries only when batting with skipper 'Tubby' Ranatunga

SANATH JAYASURIYA

When Sri Lanka won the World Cup in 1996, they did so with a completely new approach to one-day cricket. No playing yourself in – instead the openers threw the bat like there were only two overs remaining. The prime exponent was Sanath Jayasuriya, a short, balding batter promoted from the middle order. Although he has since proved himself a quality opener, he remains capable of ludicrous run-scoring feats.

Finest moment: 66 out of a first-wicket partnership of 70 with Kaluwitharana (who was out for a duck!), Singer Cup Final v Pakistan, April 1996

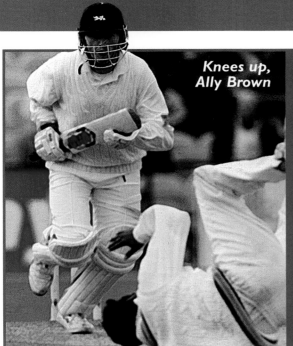

Knees up, Ally Brown

ALLY BROWN

Ally Brown does not mess about. He has tried to curb his natural aggression but it simply does not work. He is a batsman who *has* to attack. Sadly this means he will probably never play Test cricket – he is considered a little irresponsible, but he'd probably find it too dull anyway.

Finest moment: *The highest ever Sunday League score, 203 off 119 balls vs Hampshire in 1997*

If this Zulu had been at Rorke's Drift, Michael Caine's career would have been totally different

SHAHID AFRIDI

Shahid Afridi is one of several Pakistanis in recent years who have appeared older than they are. Although he has not yet played for the full Pakistan Test side, he *has* played one of the most scintillating knocks in world cricket – a century in 37 balls versus Sri Lanka in Nairobi.

Finest moment: *On his way to the fastest 100, he hit 41 in two overs – off Jayasuriya!*

MATTHEW FLEMING

Well-heeled Fleming looks every inch the Old Etonian that he is. If his background implies a disciplined, repressed individual, nothing could be further from the truth. He is one of the most adventurous cricketers today. The best evidence: his first two scoring shots in county cricket – both were sixes!

Finest moment: *Helping England to win the Sharjah tournament in 1997*

LANCE KLUSENER

When South Africa faced Australia in the World Cup semi-final in 1999, most of England wanted only one winner – neither of them. The one guy we might have felt sympathy for was 'Zulu' Klusener, who had been an unstoppable force throughout the tournament. Wielding a bat that most people would be unable to lift, he bludgeoned his way to 281 runs off only 230 balls for only twice out.

Sadly for us, he carried his form into England's tour of South Africa. One day we'll find a way to stop him.

Finest moment: *His running out of Allan Donald in the World Cup semi-final ... not!*

Right: Klusener making his name during the World Cup

BIZARRE BATTING LINE-UPS

If you like your batsmen stylish and graceful, then you may want to skip this section. The six men lined up here should carry a public health warning – they were all truly horrible to watch, yet were also strangely effective. Kids please note: these guys are not role models!

PETER WILLEY

Peter Willey should have been outlawed from the game as soon as he started his ludicrous style of standing with his back to the stumps with both feet facing the bowler. The idea was to give his dominant right eye a better sight of the ball. It was truly ugly and the ICC should have stamped on it immediately.
Best shot: *Push to mid off for a quick single*

The HORROR SHOW VI

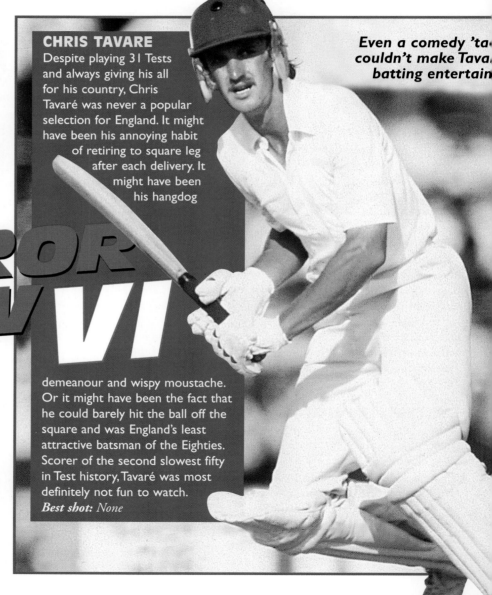

CHRIS TAVARE

Despite playing 31 Tests and always giving his all for his country, Chris Tavaré was never a popular selection for England. It might have been his annoying habit of retiring to square leg after each delivery. It might have been his hangdog demeanour and wispy moustache. Or it might have been the fact that he could barely hit the ball off the square and was England's least attractive batsman of the Eighties. Scorer of the second slowest fifty in Test history, Tavaré was most definitely not fun to watch.
Best shot: *None*

Even a comedy 'ta... couldn't make Tava... batting entertain...

JOHN CARR

After a somewhat disappointing season in 1990, John Carr retired from county cricket to take up a career in the City. He soon came back, to groans all round from the Lord's purists. Crouched at the wicket, standing face on to the bowler and with his bat held in mid-air, he looked more of a baseball slugger than a quality batsman. He proved, however, that substance is more important than style by topping the averages in 1995.
Best shot: *Smear to square leg*

CLIVE RADLEY

Clive Radley was a determined middle-order batsman who grafted and scuttled his way to over 26,000 runs in first-class cricket. Never looking comfortable at the crease, he nevertheless seemed almost impossible to get out. Always a good excuse to retire to the Tavern for a pint, only the Middlesex faithful could have enjoyed watching Radley.

Best shot: *Push to mid on for a quick single*

KEPLER WESSELS

Hard to believe, but Kepler Wessels was once a schoolboy prodigy in South Africa, mentioned in the same breath as Graeme Pollock for his free and uncomplicated style. Over the years, however, his determination to succeed led to him squeezing out almost all the fun from his game, making himself dull, dull and dull. *Wisden*, making him a Cricketer of the Year in 1995, described him thus: "He is efficient but ugly; uninteresting but packed full of substance." He would no doubt consider this a compliment.

Best shot: *Nudge past point*

This should keep that boring bugger off the pitch

JACK RUSSELL

As a wicketkeeper, Jack Russell was probably the best of his time. As a batting stylist he was quite possibly the worst. With his home-made style of defence and a maximum of three attacking shots, he often looked like he had no idea. Yet, more often than not, he managed to stick around, never failing to piss the opposition off intensely – not least because of his habit of talking to himself at the crease. A true original, his big disappointment in batting was that no one could invent a helmet shaped like a knackered old sun-hat.

Best shot: *Tickle to third man*

BIZARRE BATTING LINE-UPS

The batsman that the opposition hate the most is rarely the quickest scorer or the most talented strokemaker. Instead, he is boringly obstinate old Ronnie Reliable, the guy who sells his wicket more dearly than a full set of *Wisdens*. We may not love these guys, but we'd love to have them on our side.

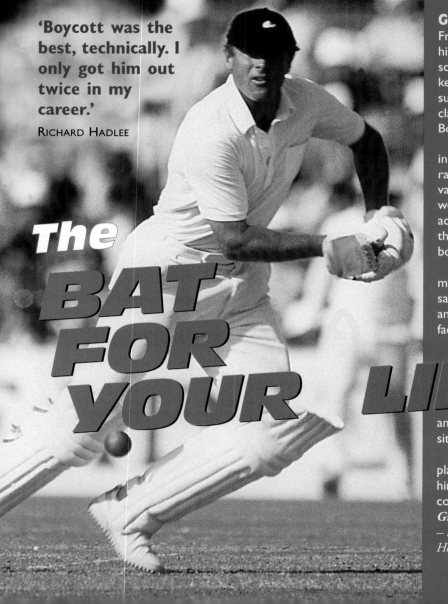

'Boycott was the best, technically. I only got him out twice in my career.'

RICHARD HADLEE

The BAT FOR YOUR LIFERS

GEOFFREY BOYCOTT

From an early age Geoffrey Boycott dedicated himself to two things and two things only – scoring as many runs as humanly possible, and keeping his average as high as possible. He succeeded in both, scoring almost 50,000 first-class runs at an average of 56.83. For Geoffrey Boycott, runs were the very currency of life itself.

Boycott could actually bat a bit, but chose early in his career to eradicate risk from his game. He rated crease occupation almost as highly as he valued runs, and developed the tightest defence in world cricket. He also developed great tactical acumen, often managing the strike to monopolise the weaker bowlers while placing himself at the bowler's end for the stronger ones.

He was notoriously selfish, particularly in the matter of run-outs, where the thought of sacrificing himself to save a team-mate was anathema. He would frequently go AWOL when faced with a dangerous attack or a dodgy pitch, and would rarely throw the bat even when the situation demanded quick runs.

But, despite it all, he was the one England player you could rely on. And, even if only to stop him sticking his bloody car keys in the pitch, we could do with him now.

Greatest innings: 191 vs Australia at Headingley '77 – his 100th hundred, at home against the old enemy. *Hollywood couldn't have scripted it better*

> Ah'll tell thee what, mi gran could bat all t'day on this pitch – thi dunt mek wiggets like thi used to tha knows – if any o' them English batsmen mek less than 200 on this thi want lockin oop – ah could've batted a week wi a golf club if there were any booger good enough to last that long in't middle wi me (etc for five days)

SUNIL GAVASKAR

The little master, Sunil Gavaskar, was a ruthless accumulator of runs who could add 50 to his score without you really noticing. Amazingly, he scored a Test century once every seven innings. No opposition or situation was beyond him. His game was founded on impeccable defence, though maybe he took it too far in his first World Cup knock – when he scored a mere 36 not out in 60 overs!

Greatest innings: 102 vs West Indies at Port of Spain, 1976 – part of highest-ever fourth innings winning total of 406-4

KEN BARRINGTON

Ken Barrington was not pretty, but you would go a long way to find a more effective batter. He scored Test centuries at every English Test ground and in every Test-playing country. Indeed when he retired prematurely from Tests aged 39, he did so with an average of 58.67, exceeded only by Sutcliffe of comparable run-scorers. Popular inside and outside the game, his early death aged 50 robbed cricket of a much-loved character.

Greatest innings: 142 vs Pakistan at The Oval, 1967 – his 19th Test century, but his first at his beloved home ground

55

GLENN TURNER

At a time when New Zealand generally found it difficult to draw Tests, never mind win them, one player stood out like a flying kiwi in a decidedly earthbound flock. Glenn Turner had most of the shots, but chose to use them sparingly, concentrating instead on staying in. His nickname became 'minibus', as he carried ten passengers so frequently and yet never flagged. Rarely on a winning Test side, he nevertheless won many admirers.

Greatest innings: 141 not out vs Glamorgan at Swansea in 1977 – scored out of a total of 169 all out with the next highest score being 7

Caution, wide load...
Glenn Turner – a posterior built for posterity

LEN HUTTON

Len Hutton was, for a period of time after the retirement of Bradman, the best batsman in world cricket. His career, which was thriving before the Second World War, blossomed after it, despite the loss after an accident of two inches of his left arm. He was certainly England's best batsman for most of his career, and it was felt that "if Len failed, the chances were that England would". Fortunately he rarely did.

Greatest innings: 205 vs West Indies at Sabina Park, 1954 – batted with grim determination to lead England to a series saving win in the Final Test

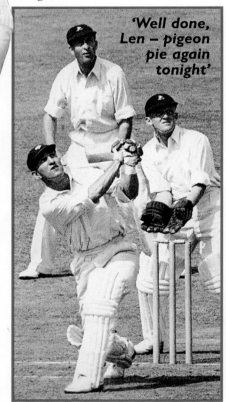

'Well done, Len – pigeon pie again tonight'

STEVE WAUGH

Steve Waugh is the most competitive player in cricket today. He has a fierce will to win, and a Scrooge-like determination to give absolutely nothing away. He has been Australia's match-winner or saver so many times it does not bear thinking about. If only he had been born in England…

Greatest innings: 200 vs West Indies at Kingston, 1995 – his 231 partnership with brother Mark led to the Windies' first series defeat in 15 years

This means Waugh… Steve blows a hole in the opposition again

…AND THE STYLISH VI, LED BY THE MAN WHOSE LIFE IS ONE LONG CHAMPAGNE MOMENT

'It's awfully tiresome, old boy, but that chap Lillee is waiting to bowl and the bounder doesn't even like Moët…'

'What a princely entry! The boy has class.'
JOHN ARLOTT AFTER GOWER DESPATCHED HIS FIRST BALL IN TEST CRICKET TO THE BOUNDARY

1. David Gower
2. Peter May
3. Tom Graveney
4. Aravinda Da Silva
5. Ted Dexter
6. Greg Chappell

BIZARRE BATTING LINE-UPS

Anyone who has ever gone out to bat will, at some point, have suffered from 'rushofblooditis'. This can manifest itself in many ways, from the cross-bat swipe when your team need you to shut up shop to the rash goading of the opposition's fastest bowler. The six batters below have all distinguished themselves with some act of senseless stupidity and we hereby salute them.

The MOMENT OF MADNESS VI

'How am I doing, Thorpey?'

'Too bloody well, son'

GRAHAM THORPE

Whether this is a moment of madness or selfishness is debatable. With England chasing 208 to beat the Kiwis in the First Test in 1999, Alex Tudor came in as nightwatchman. Next day, the youngster proved a revelation, playing attractively to take England within a whisker of victory and himself to the brink of 100. With seven wickets in hand, we all expected his partner – county colleague Graham Thorpe – to help him make his first (and possibly only) Test century. But no. Thorpe set off as though he had a train to catch and left Tudor five short of his ton with only one run needed for victory. Tudor hit a four, but ended on 99 not out. Thorpe was unapologetic, but if I were him I wouldn't spend too much time in the nets when Tudor is bowling.

STEVE WAUGH

Steve Waugh, the iceman, had a rare rush of blood in at the MCG on England's tour of 1998/9. Australia needed just 175 to win, and at 130 for three with the Waugh twins together the game was up. But suddenly Dean Headley transformed himself into a world-beater and four wickets fell for 10 runs. Yet Waugh was still in, and took Australia to within 14 runs of victory. Headley managed to take Nicholson, but still Waugh was there and ready to face a tiring Gough.

He could have shielded his tail-end partner, but inexplicably chose to take a run off the first ball. It was a massive gamble that backfired spectacularly, as Gough ripped out MacGill first ball followed by McGrath two balls later to give England a famous 12-run victory.

LANCE KLUSENER

In the 1999 World Cup, the strongest teams were South Africa and Australia. Having already played out one epic contest, they came together in the semifinal. The match had swung one way then the next, and was on a knife edge as the final over commenced with South Africa needing nine with one wicket left.

Yet again, Klusener changed the complexion of the game by smashing Fleming's first two balls to the boundary.

The scores were now tied and it seemed inconceivable that the Springboks would not score the one run required off the last four balls. The third, however, was a dot ball. With everyone's nerves jangling, Klusener faced the fourth.

He had obviously decided to charge come what may, but failed to inform his partner, Allan Donald. Donald was run out and Australia went into the Final, which they won. A sad end for the player of the tournament.

GEOFFREY BOYCOTT

'Sir' Geoff was famous for his abysmal running between the wickets. In 1977 he returned to Test cricket after a self-inflicted absence of three years, and found himself batting against Australia at Trent Bridge with local hero Derek Randall. Arkle looked in great form – but didn't bargain on Boycott's eccentric running. Boycs called for an impossible single and Randall unselfishly gave up his wicket. For once, Boycott looked genuinely ashamed. He redeemed himself by scoring a century and 80 to lead England to victory, but was never forgiven by the Notts faithful.

CHRIS BROAD

In 1986/7 Chris Broad was International Cricketer of the Year. In 1987/8 he was Spoilt Brat of the Year. Against Pakistan in Lahore, Broad was given out caught off Iqbal Qasim. So incensed was he by the decision that he refused to go, standing his ground

MIKE GATTING

England have reached the World Cup Final three times, but sadly have always ended up the loser. Their best chance of winning was in 1987, when Mike Gatting's team took on Australia. The Aussies had posted a good target of 253 in 50 overs, but England were going well at 135 for two off 31 overs. With Gatting and Athey both well set, Allan Border was short of options. His last gamble was to bring himself on to bowl his inoffensive left arm spin.

Interestingly, part of his thinking was that Gatting would start to play it safe, determined not to get out to his very average bowling. He was wrong.

Gatting decided well before Border's first ball was bowled that he was going to play the reverse sweep. Border dragged the ball down the leg side, Gatting got a top edge on to his shoulder, and the ball ballooned in the air for an easy catch to the keeper, Greg Dyer. England went on to lose and eventually become the laughing stock of world cricket ... and it's all your fault, Mike!!

for a full minute before Graham Gooch persuaded him to leave. Later that winter, against Australia in the Bicentennial Test at Sydney, Broad reacted to his dismissal (having scored a rather fortunate 139) by smashing his stumps with his bat. I'm sure we've all wanted to do this at some point, but in a celebration Test match? Not quite the done thing, old boy.

YOU'RE NOT AS GOOD AS YOUR DAD XI

John Bradsen, an Adelaide lecturer, hit the headlines in 2000 by changing his name back to the one he was born with ... Bradman. For 30 years John had tried to escape being 'son of the greatest cricketer ever', but at 61 years old he finally bowed to the inevitable.

Being the son of a famous cricketer can't be easy. You have two choices – either make your career in a totally different field (cowardly) or play cricket and try to exceed your father's deeds (stupid).

We pick here an eleven who have followed in Dad's footsteps, and assess who would win the battle of the generations. Sadly, it's often pater who wins the generation game.

Left: Sir Colin Cowdrey – a hard act to follow, as Chris discovered

FATHER	SON

ALAN BUTCHER
- Looked bad, scored well
- Has one solitary cap
- Played until age of 44

MARK BUTCHER
- Looks good, scores bugger-all
- Mystifyingly has lots of England caps
- Ex-England skipper's brother-in-law

VERDICT: PHOTO FINISH, UNABLE TO SEPARATE

HANIF MOHAMMAD
- 55 Tests, averaged 44
- Top score of 499 not out
- Also made longest ever Test innings

SHOAIB MOHAMMAD
- 45 Tests, also averaged 44 (spooky!)
- Top Test score a pathetic 203 not out
- Joke bowler, took 2 in 2 overs v Windies

VERDICT: DAD, FOR PERSISTENCE

MICKY STEWART
- Eight Tests
- Great close fielder
- Decent England coach

ALEC STEWART
- Most Test runs in the 1990s
- Reliable wicketkeeper
- True Brit, helmet kisser (not <u>that</u> helmet)

VERDICT: SON, BY A FEW LENGTHS

SIR LEN HUTTON
- 79 Tests over three decades
- Legendary opening bat
- Averaged over 56 in Tests

RICHARD HUTTON
- Five Tests in 1971
- Useful all-rounder
- Got a bit too posh for Yorkshire

VERDICT: DAD, BY A DISTANCE

SIR COLIN COWDREY
- Over 100 Tests for England
- Masterly batsman and slip fielder
- Initials spell MCC

CHRIS COWDREY
- Six Tests in 1984-8
- Useless all-rounder
- Shortest-lived England captain

VERDICT: DAD, BY A COUNTRY MILE

ALAN EALHAM
- Decent middle order batsman
- Legendary cover fielder
- Uncapped, but might have been

MARK EALHAM
- Feisty all-rounder
- Hard-hitting one-day batsman
- Not quite up to a regular Test slot

VERDICT: SON, BY A SHORT HEAD

FATHER	SON

ALAN KNOTT
- Genius Kent and England keeper
- Annoying, inventive batsman
- Scored 135 in a Test match

JAMES KNOTT
- Up-and-coming keeper
- Born in Kent, plays for Surrey
- Middle name Alan

VERDICT: GIVE UP SON, YOUR DAD IS A LIVING LEGEND

IAN BOTHAM
- Took a few wickets, made a few runs, made a few catches, took a little pot
- Played football for Scunthorpe
- Slightly fat

LIAM BOTHAM
- Took five wickets in an innings on first appearance in first-class cricket
- Top-class rugby player
- Extremely athletic

VERDICT: GOOD DECISION TO CONCENTRATE ON RUGBY, LIAM

LANCE CAIRNS
- Bowled the biggest in-swingers ever
- Played with a funny-shaped bat
- Hit the ball miles

CHRIS CAIRNS
- Can bat a bit and bowl a bit
- Superb slower ball (ask Chris Read)
- Handsome dog

VERDICT: SON, BY A COUPLE OF LENGTHS

PETER POLLOCK
- 28 Tests for South Africa
- 116 wickets at 16
- Graeme's brother

SHAUN POLLOCK
- Sometime world No.1 ranked bowler
- Useful late order batter
- Richie 'Happy Days' Cunningham lookalike

VERDICT: SON, BY A SHORT, GINGER HEAD

ARNIE SIDEBOTTOM
- Hard-working Yorkshire paceman
- Looks born to be called Sidebottom
- Played football for Man United

RYAN SIDEBOTTOM
- Rising Yorkshire paceman
- Looks too cool for a Sidebottom
- Has impressive big hair

VERDICT: DAD, FOR BEING MORE AUTHENTICALLY YORKSHIRE

OVERALL SCORE: DADS 6, SONS 4, NO RESULT 1

Uh-oh, Randall's broken into Gower's champagne cellar again…

The MAVERICK XI

If we all took a step back from the game that we love so much, we would have to admit that cricket is an unusual game. It takes an inordinately long time, contains numerous rules and customs that are basically impenetrable, and can frequently be infuriatingly unrewarding.

As a batter, you can field all day then go out to bat and be out first ball.

As a fielder, you can stand in eight different positions and still not have a single ball hit in your direction.

And as a bowler you can bowl your best spell for 0-50 and your worst for 3-21.

Not surprising, then, that cricket has attracted to both its playing and its spectating ranks a higher than average number of unusual characters.

We feature XI of the best here, ranging from devil-may-care cavaliers to those who dared to be different, plus a few characters who are just plain odd.

Opposite: The unpredictable Mr Randall – they don't make 'em like that any more

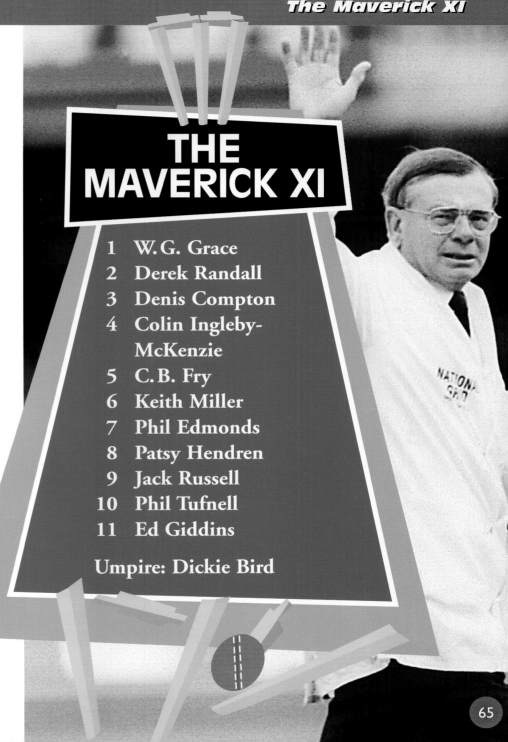

THE MAVERICK XI

1 W. G. Grace
2 Derek Randall
3 Denis Compton
4 Colin Ingleby-McKenzie
5 C. B. Fry
6 Keith Miller
7 Phil Edmonds
8 Patsy Hendren
9 Jack Russell
10 Phil Tufnell
11 Ed Giddins

Umpire: Dickie Bird

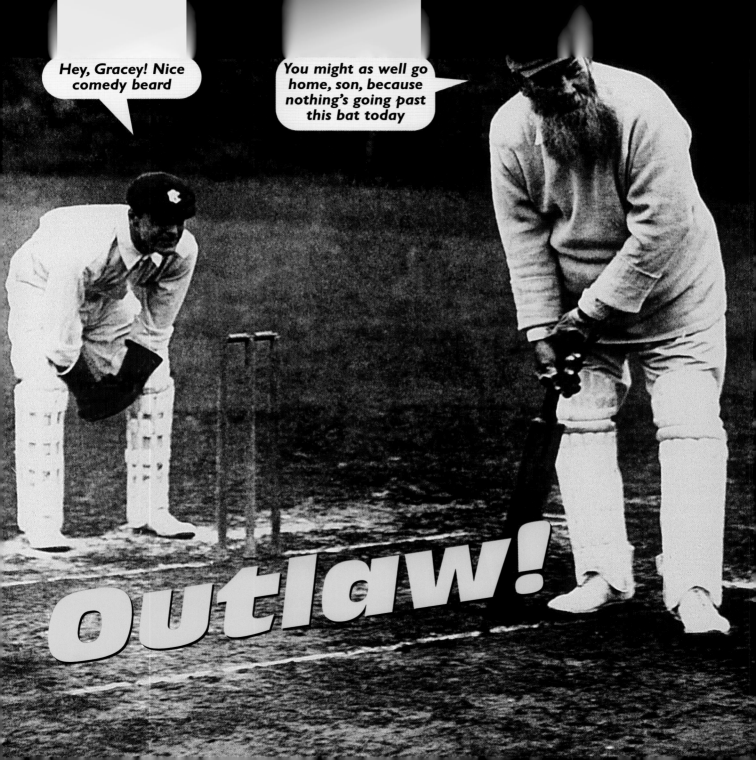

W. G. GRACE

Dr William Gilbert Grace dominated 19th-century cricket and he knew it. While other players tended to abide by the rules of the game, the Doctor was an unrepentant sporting outlaw.

One famous victim of this cricketing highwayman was the umpire who gave him out early in an innings. "They've come to watch me bat, not you umpiring," he announced imperiously, before replacing the bails and continuing his innings.

Ferociously competitive, Grace would seize any chance to increase his score. On one occasion, the ball stuck in his pad. He promptly set off for the boundary, crossed the ropes, and dislodged the ball for a six! Another time, the ball lodged in the folds of his shirt – and he refused to stop and hand over the ball until he had completed six all run.

Then there was the towering hit into the outfield during a county match. After completing a run with the ball still in the air, it became clear that he was about to be caught – so W. G. instantly declared the innings. Somehow he managed to persuade the umpire not only to give him not out, but also to allow the first-run single to stand.

Grace made another surprise declaration in 1893 when he closed his team's innings with his own score on 93. Bystanders were bemused – until W. G. revealed that 93 was the only score between 0 and 100 that he had not yet recorded.

W.G. could always bat against the best ... even with a pillow stuck down his trousers

> 'To watch Denis Compton play cricket on a good day was to know what joy was. I think I made the right choice.'
> – JOHN MAJOR AFTER ATTENDING COMPTON'S MEMORIAL SERVICE RATHER THAN THE HANDOVER OF HONG KONG

Brylcreem boy!

DENIS COMPTON

Denis Compton was *the* hero of the Forties and early Fifties for many sports followers. Not merely a brilliant cricketer for Middlesex and England, he was also a top-class football winger who won the League and FA Cup with Arsenal. But above all he was also a truly charismatic personality who illuminated the drab post-war period and, indeed, the war itself.

Compton did not believe in practice or pre-match preparation, frequently turning up for matches without his kit and wearing a dinner suit from the night before. He was so in control of his batting that he would often toy with the opposition, responding to field changes by hitting the ball to where the fielder had just been removed. In his pomp it seemed that Denis could do anything.

DEREK RANDALL

With English cricket desperately short of characters, what would we give for another Derek Randall now? Randall was a true one-off. He showed uninhibited enjoyment in his cricket – a joyous handspring as England clinched the Ashes in 1977, fielding in a policeman's helmet in India… But he was also skilful and determined, and scored the slowest century in Ashes Tests in 1978/9 to help clinch the series.

Randall will be remembered most for his great innings of 174 in the Centenary Test of 1977. His eccentricity was given full expression in his time at the crease – his constant talking to himself, doffing his cap to the snarling Lillee, smiling and laughing throughout … but all the while delivering the goods.

Gambling man!

COLIN INGLEBY-MCKENZIE

The flamboyant captain of Hampshire, who led his county to the Championship in 1961, was also keen on the horses. On one occasion, he actually stopped a game at Lord's between MCC and Yorkshire so that he could go to the boundary fence, where he spent the next three minutes listening to live radio commentary of the St Leger. Sadly, his horse was unplaced.

Ingleby-McKenzie ruled his side with fun rather than iron discipline. Explaining the secret of his championship success in 1961, he claimed: "I always insist my team are in bed by ten o'clock; after all, play starts at half past eleven."

Left: Ingleby-McKenzie's horse was obviously struggling in the 2.30

KEITH MILLER

Alongside Denis Compton, Keith Miller is probably the most enduring cricketing hero of the last 60 years. Tall, strong and handsome, Miller was Botham before Botham – an all-rounder who excelled in all aspects of the game, an ultra-competitive match-winner and a man of immense charisma.

Like Compton, Miller believed in having fun while playing and in having lots more fun while not playing. He once

King

turned up late for a game he was skippering. As he hurriedly took to the pitch, he was alerted to the fact that he was taking the field with a team of 12. Without breaking stride he turned to the team and called out "All right, one of you guys disappear." The team decided that the youngest should go … so they took the field without their wicketkeeper!

C.B.FRY

To call C.B.Fry a maverick is probably to do him an injustice. He was certainly one of the most all-round talented individuals the world has ever known.

In cricket he pioneered mobile footwork and scored 30,000 runs (including centuries in six consecutive innings, which remains a record) at an average over 50. He represented his country at football, held the world long jump record for 21 years, was a top-class hunter and fisher … and could basically do everything. Outside of sport, he was academically brilliant, and achieved great things in many spheres. He was even offered the throne of Albania. He was, in short … a bastard!

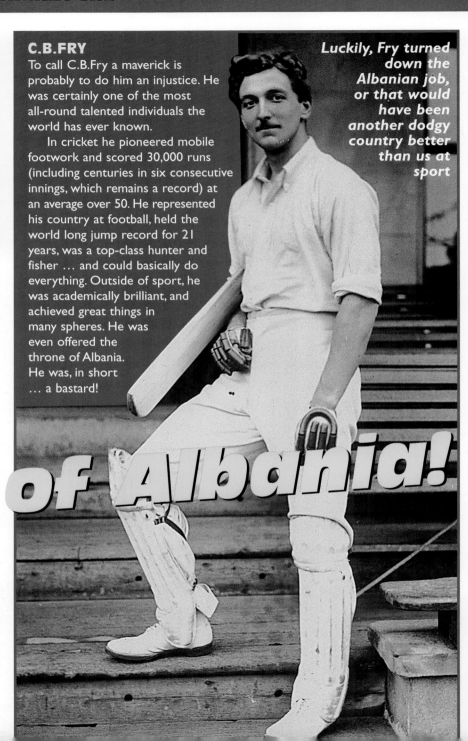

Luckily, Fry turned down the Albanian job, or that would have been another dodgy country better than us at sport

of Albania!

PHIL EDMONDS

Nowadays a mobile phone is standard equipment for all sportsman, but twas not ever thus. Hence, when Phil Edmonds started appearing on the Lord's balcony padded up and with phone in hand, it caused something of a stir.

Edmonds, it transpired, was coolly conducting serious business deals while his teammates played cards and listened to their Walkmans.

The Middlesex and England slow bowler was always his own man, in the habit of having a lie down during play and often to be seen having a read of a spectator's newspaper. Odd that he was never made captain.

Edmonds enjoys another good day on the Stock Exchange as his team-mates endure a tough day in the field

PATSY HENDREN

It was said of Elias 'Patsy' Hendren that "no game in which he was engaged could be altogether dull". Always the life and soul of the party, he was a first-rate mimic and wit, and would conjure up some stunt or other during dull periods in play to keep fans amused. Funnily enough, like the mischievous Mr Edmonds, he also played for Middlesex.

Hendren played in over 50 Tests for England in the Twenties and Thirties, alongside such colossal figures as Walter Hammond, Herbert Sutcliffe and Jack Hobbs, and he outscored all but Hobbs. But Hendren still found time for fun – epitomised by his arrival at the crease against the West Indies at Lord's in 1933. Hendren was correct in all details … except that he was sporting a deerstalker hat. He claimed it had been fashioned by his wife to protect his head from damage, but many felt that it was simply a gag.

Businessman!

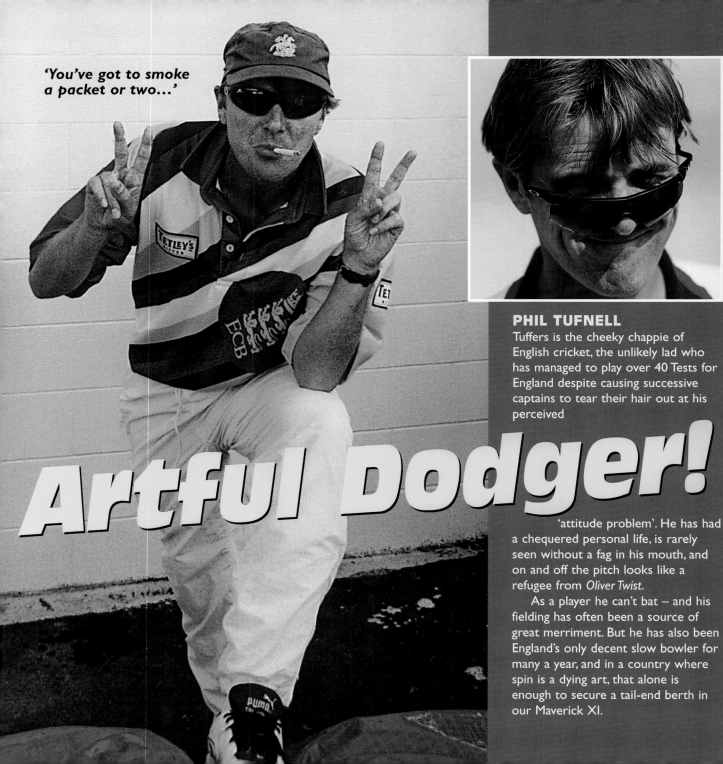

'You've got to smoke a packet or two...'

Artful Dodger!

PHIL TUFNELL

Tuffers is the cheeky chappie of English cricket, the unlikely lad who has managed to play over 40 Tests for England despite causing successive captains to tear their hair out at his perceived 'attitude problem'. He has had a chequered personal life, is rarely seen without a fag in his mouth, and on and off the pitch looks like a refugee from *Oliver Twist*.

As a player he can't bat — and his fielding has often been a source of great merriment. But he has also been England's only decent slow bowler for many a year, and in a country where spin is a dying art, that alone is enough to secure a tail-end berth in our Maverick XI.

Ed Giddins was no-balled by the TCCB for hitting the white lines once too often

charlie!

JACK RUSSELL

Wicketkeepers are a singular breed and Russell is one of the most singular. The Gloucestershire and England keeper has worn the same battered sun hat for years, avoids foreign food on tour and eats only steak and chips … every day.

Jack is also a talented water-colour painter – surely a unique occupation for a Test cricketer.

ED GIDDINS

Drugs in sport is a major social issue … except in cricket. The game is so odd that no single drug could possibly be perform-ance enhancing. Ed Giddins' performance was certainly not enhanced by the 20-month ban handed down by the TCCB after he tested positive for cocaine in 1996. It did, however, confer 'lad' status on naughty Giddins, and didn't do his career too much harm, as he played for England soon after his return to the game. Never-theless, you've got to say he's a bit of a charlie.

73

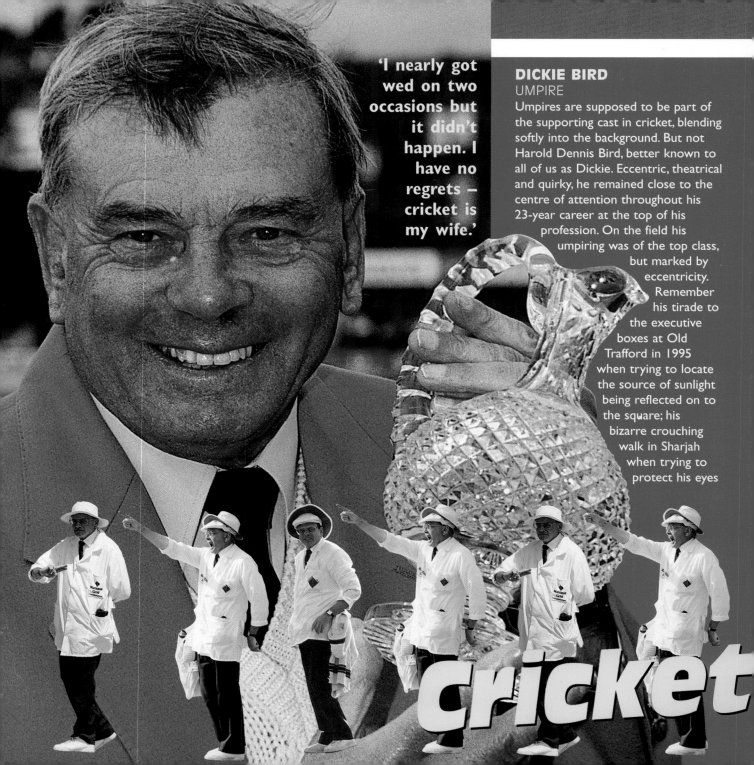

'I nearly got wed on two occasions but it didn't happen. I have no regrets – cricket is my wife.'

DICKIE BIRD
UMPIRE

Umpires are supposed to be part of the supporting cast in cricket, blending softly into the background. But not Harold Dennis Bird, better known to all of us as Dickie. Eccentric, theatrical and quirky, he remained close to the centre of attention throughout his 23-year career at the top of his profession. On the field his umpiring was of the top class, but marked by eccentricity. Remember his tirade to the executive boxes at Old Trafford in 1995 when trying to locate the source of sunlight being reflected on to the square; his bizarre crouching walk in Sharjah when trying to protect his eyes

cricket

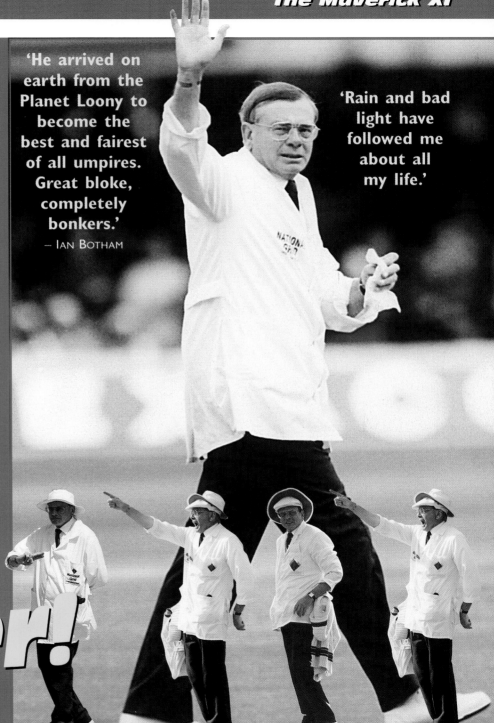

from the sun; his many hunched runs to the boundary to berate some spectator moving behind the bowler's arm… and, of course, his famed ability to turn a clear sunny day into a dank, miserable, rainy one.

Off the field, his foibles are well-documented: his excessively early arrivals for matches, sometimes getting to the ground before the groundstaff had opened up; his domestic ineptitude (he is still looked after by his sister); his non-stop chatter; and his ability to attract a continual stream of minor disasters…

But he remains one of cricket's best loved characters, by players and fans alike. His final Test at Lord's in 1996 was marked by a huge outpouring of affection and emotion. It says everything about Bird that after wiping the tears from his eyes, he settled down to umpire and five balls into the innings gave a rock-solid decision for lbw against Mike Atherton. For all of his idiosyncrasies, he was the real article as an umpire.

'He arrived on earth from the Planet Loony to become the best and fairest of all umpires. Great bloke, completely bonkers.'
— IAN BOTHAM

'Rain and bad light have followed me about all my life.'

nutter!

*Graham Gooch:
Squeaky voice,
tough guy*

The
HARD
XI

There is a certain breed of cricketer who can be relied upon in all situations, who withstands all the slings and arrows of outrageous fortune, the man the rest of the team looks to in times of trial.

This cricketer, whose head will never drop and whose spirit will never flag, is the true competitor. He may be tough physically; he may show his mettle in a mental way. But, in whatever fashion, he is simply nails.

Of late, few such men have been English, sadly, but we still pay homage here to the Hard XI.

Will Curtly roll over? Nope, he'll just blow England away

THE HARD XI

1	Graham Gooch
2	Brian Close
3	Stan McCabe
4	Javed Miandad
5	Dean Jones
6	Ian Chappell
7	Ian Healy
8	Curtly Ambrose
9	Glenn McGrath
10	Fred Trueman
11	Angus Fraser

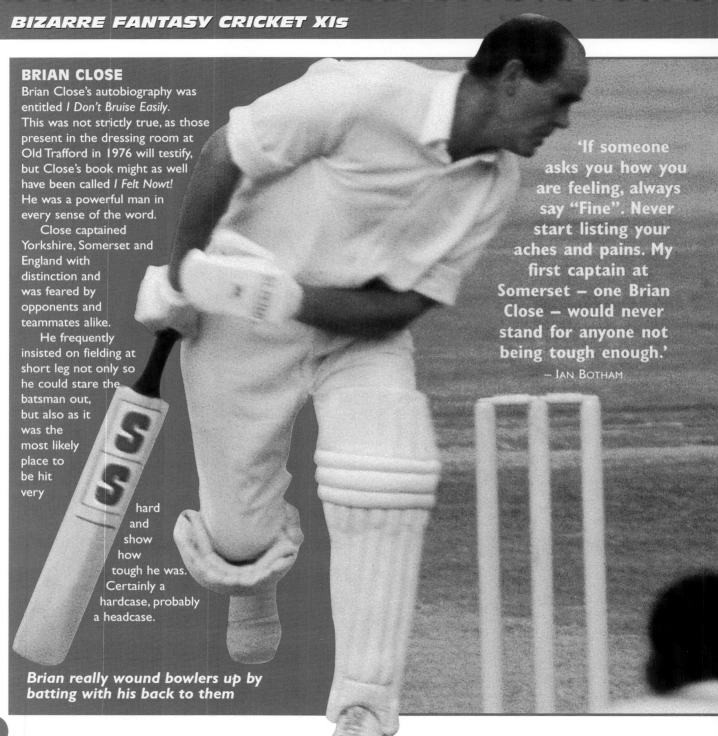

BRIAN CLOSE

Brian Close's autobiography was entitled *I Don't Bruise Easily*. This was not strictly true, as those present in the dressing room at Old Trafford in 1976 will testify, but Close's book might as well have been called *I Felt Nowt!* He was a powerful man in every sense of the word.

Close captained Yorkshire, Somerset and England with distinction and was feared by opponents and teammates alike.

He frequently insisted on fielding at short leg not only so he could stare the batsman out, but also as it was the most likely place to be hit very hard and show how tough he was. Certainly a hardcase, probably a headcase.

'If someone asks you how you are feeling, always say "Fine". Never start listing your aches and pains. My first captain at Somerset – one Brian Close – would never stand for anyone not being tough enough.'
– IAN BOTHAM

Brian really wound bowlers up by batting with his back to them

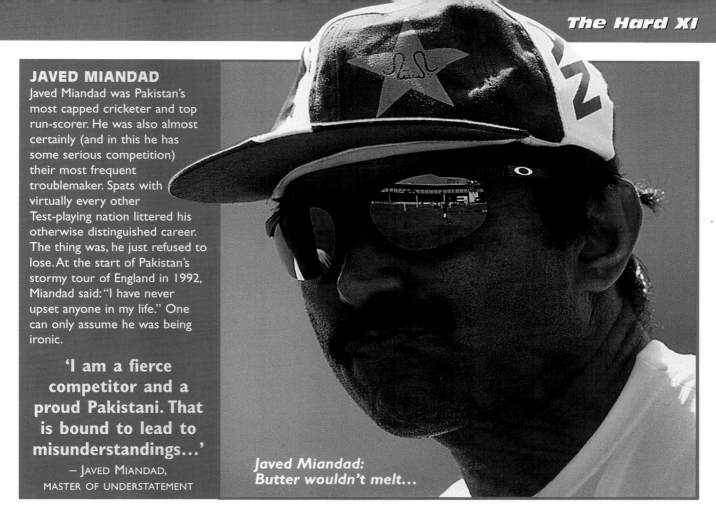

JAVED MIANDAD

Javed Miandad was Pakistan's most capped cricketer and top run-scorer. He was also almost certainly (and in this he has some serious competition) their most frequent troublemaker. Spats with virtually every other Test-playing nation littered his otherwise distinguished career. The thing was, he just refused to lose. At the start of Pakistan's stormy tour of England in 1992, Miandad said: "I have never upset anyone in my life." One can only assume he was being ironic.

> **'I am a fierce competitor and a proud Pakistani. That is bound to lead to misunderstandings...'**
> – JAVED MIANDAD,
> MASTER OF UNDERSTATEMENT

Javed Miandad:
Butter wouldn't melt...

GRAHAM GOOCH

If Graham Gooch looked as weighed down as Atlas in his years as England captain, who could blame him? Often, Gooch's obduracy was all that stood between his team and ignominy. His tough training regime caused several star contemporaries to retire to the safety of the commentary box. But Gooch plodded relentlessly on, notably taking on Ambrose and Walsh at Headingley in 1991 with a courageous 154 not out to end West Indian dominance over England.

STAN McCABE

Stan McCabe, who played for Australia from 1930 to 1938, was not only a very good batsman, he was also a very brave one. He exemplified this during the Bodyline tour of 1932/3, when he hit 385 runs in the five Tests, averaging 43.

McCabe's finest hour was his 187 not out in the First Test, made out of a total of 278. He hit 25 fours, including many hooked – yes, hooked – off the ferocious assault of Larwood and Voce. True courage.

DEAN JONES

Dean Jones joined the pantheon of legendary Aussie tough guys on his first tour to India in 1986/7. In only his fifth Test he scored a remarkable 210 not out in the tied first Test, overcoming frequent bouts of nausea and leg cramps in the intense heat.

Needless to say, he got a lot of sympathy from the Australian captain, Allan Border, who refused to believe that Jones was really ill, even when he was carted off to hospital to recover.

IAN HEALY

In its profile of Ian Healy as one of its Cricketers of the Year in 1994, *Wisden* described him as a 'gloves-off cricketer' – an odd description for a keeper, but completely appropriate in Healy's case. Healy was a total competitor, fierce in his belief that mental and physical toughness, allied to raw competitiveness were the most admirable qualities in a sportsman. He was also lippy, and many wanted him to fall flat on his face. Sadly for England in particular, he rarely did, maintaining high standards behind the stumps and being annoyingly effective in front.

'I can take these Poms on kneeling down'

CURTLY AMBROSE

The sight of Curtly Ambrose thundering in towards the wicket must fill any batsman in the world with trepidation. Six foot seven inches tall, capable of propelling the ball at 90 miles an hour and devastatingly accurate, Ambrose can hit you anywhere he wants.

A quiet man off the pitch, he shows great aggression on it. His appealing is fearsome and his celebration of wicket-taking second to none. If only we made 'em like that in this country.

IAN CHAPPELL

It is a little unfair to lay the blame for the decline of manners in modern cricket at the door of one man, but Ian Chappell as captain of Australia certainly did a lot to hasten their demise. He inherited a listless side that had been beaten at home by England, and set about turning them into a formidable, ruthless, successful team. He encouraged sledging, not walking, excessive appealing and intimidatory bowling – all now ingrained into Aussie cricketing culture. Unfortunately he also encouraged another trait that is equally ingrained into Australian cricket … winning.

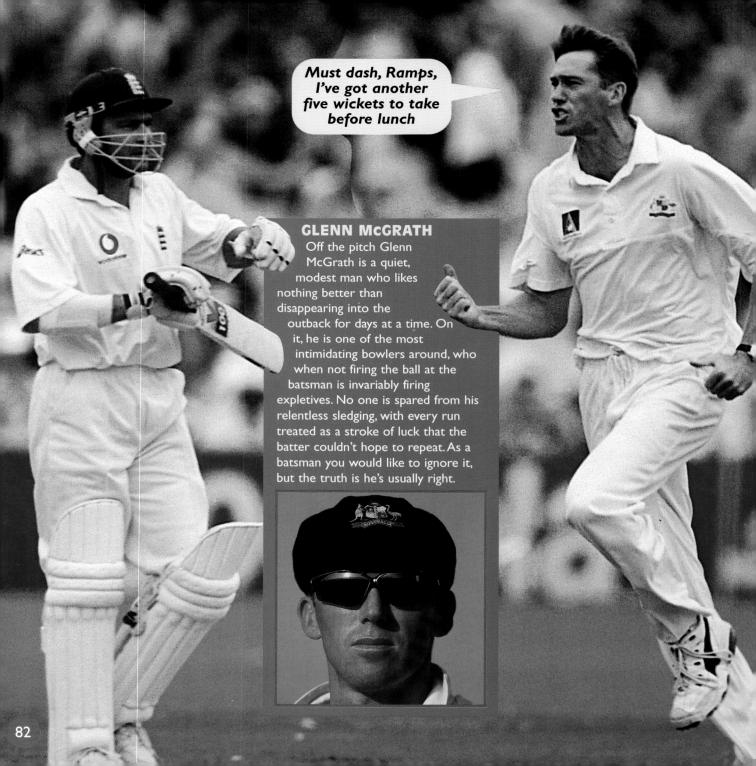

Must dash, Ramps, I've got another five wickets to take before lunch

GLENN McGRATH

Off the pitch Glenn McGrath is a quiet, modest man who likes nothing better than disappearing into the outback for days at a time. On it, he is one of the most intimidating bowlers around, who when not firing the ball at the batsman is invariably firing expletives. No one is spared from his relentless sledging, with every run treated as a stroke of luck that the batter couldn't hope to repeat. As a batsman you would like to ignore it, but the truth is he's usually right.

FRED TRUEMAN

Frederick Sewards Trueman was an ultra-competitive Yorkshireman who lived up to the soubriquet 'Fiery Fred' both on and off the pitch. As a bowler he was passionate and wholehearted, and intimidated all batsmen with his aggressive approach. He was naturally fast, but augmented this with great skill and subtlety, his slower off-cutter being a particularly deadly weapon.

Off the pitch he was never afraid to speak his mind – and this, allied to his unwillingness to bow to authority, meant he missed several Tests that he really should have been selected for. Despite this, he still became the first player to take 300 wickets in Tests.

If he is much missed by England, he is more so by Yorkshire. With Fred, the White Rose won the Championship seven times. It hasn't won it once since.

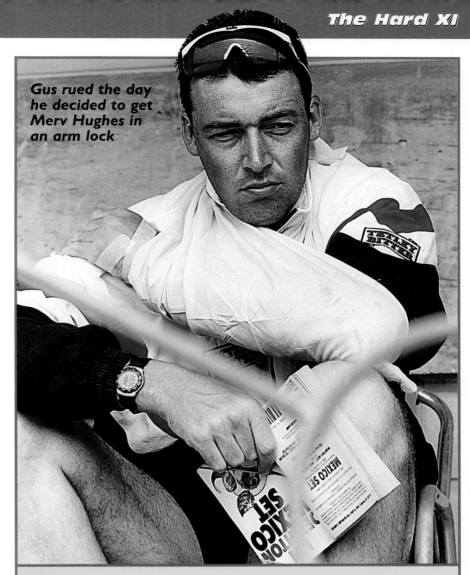

Gus rued the day he decided to get Merv Hughes in an arm lock

Yes, grumpy old Fred really was a matinée idol in the Fifties

ANGUS FRASER

One of England's unlikeliest heroes in recent years has been the unathletic and unhealthy-looking Angus Fraser. Fraser, who manages to appear knackered walking from third man to hand over his sweater, was England's most determined bowler of the 1990s. He simply never gave up, and ran in ball after ball determined to give nothing away and make the batsman play at everything. For having come back in style from serious injury and from being dropped several times by his country he takes a rare English place in this XI.

Cricket appears a civilised game – hundreds of years of history, a culture of rules and regulations, beautifully manicured pitches, pristine white kit, umpires. But beneath the surface, like in a good David Lynch film, there lurks an underbelly of malpractice and skullduggery. In this team we feature eleven players who created scandal. Whilst some remained within the rules of the game, most behaved well outside the spirit. They are the Controversy XI.

Dermot Reeve – a man who'd travel to the ends of the earth in search of a bit of aggro

THE CONTROVERSY XI

1 **Mike Gatting**
2 **Brian Rose**
3 **Trevor Chappell**
4 **Arjuna Ranatunga**
5 **Dermot Reeve**
6 **Douglas Jardine**
7 **Rodney Marsh**
8 **Dennis Lillee**
9 **Tony Greig**
10 **Aftab Gul**
11 **Basil d'Oliveira**

MIKE GATTING
SHAKOOR RANA'S VERY BEST PAL

For years there had been questions about the impartiality of Pakistani umpires in Pakistan – and on England's tour of 1987/8, even more questions were asked than normal. In short, the umpiring was diabolical.

It was all too much for England skipper Mike Gatting, and in the Second Test at Faisalabad the wheels well and truly fell off. Umpire Shakoor Rana accused Gatting of cheating when he moved a fielder behind the batsman's back, and a heated debate ensued. As *Wisden* reported: "The language employed throughout the discourse was basic."

Rana refused to officiate until Gatting apologised, which he finally did, most grudgingly, in a scruffy handwritten note:

Dear Shakoor Rana
I apologise for the bad language used during the 2nd day of the Test Match at Fisalabad (sic). – Mike Gatting

By then, a day's play had been missed. The game was drawn, Pakistan won the series 1-0, and Rana became a national hero.

As for Gatting, in the following months he seemed to go looking for trouble. In 1988 he was stripped of the England captaincy after he invited a barmaid to his hotel room to celebrate his birthday ... in the middle of a Test match in which he was not-out overnight.

Then in 1990 he led a doomed rebel tour to South Africa, during which Nelson Mandela was freed. By the time protests forced Gatting & Co to go home with their tails between their legs, his brilliant 1986/7 Ashes win in Australia and subsequent OBE were a long-forgotten memory.

Gatting tries for that sophisticated David Gower look, in the hope that some of it rubs off on his batting

"TROUBLE? ME? SURELY NOT..."

'I agree I went too far with Shakoor Rana, but he started swearing at me and calling me a cheat. I just snapped. You can only take so much.'

GATTING, PICTURED WITH RANA AND ENGLAND TOUR MANAGER PETER LUSH

"F***ing cheating c***!"
– Shakoor Rana's outburst which started it all

"Pakistan have been cheating us for 37 years and it is getting worse. It was bad enough when I toured Pakistan in 1951."
– Tom Graveney, 1988

"I'm not surprised the whole of Pakistan is proud of Shakoor. He will rank with Hanif, Zaheer and Imran for his 'contributions' to Pakistan cricket." – Sunil Gavaskar, 1988

"We don't know anything about the two guys appointed, but we believe they will be better than having two Pakistani umpires."
– Martin Crowe of New Zealand, approving the decision to appoint neutral umpires for the 1990 series. The Pakistani board were so offended they reversed the decision

TREVOR CHAPPELL
UNDERARM AND UNDERHAND

Trevor Chappell was an all-rounder good enough to play three Tests for Australia – but he will go down in history as the scoundrel who bowled underarm to prevent New Zealand winning a one-day international in 1981.

Under orders from his brother Greg, Trevor rolled the ball along the ground to give batsman Brian McKechnie no chance of scoring the six required from the last ball. New Zealanders were so annoyed, they almost got cross. Chappell was forgiven, but never forgotten.

BRIAN ROSE
CONNIVING CAPTAIN

In 1979, Somerset's final B&H Cup group match was at Worcester. Somerset – two points ahead in the table – would go through even if they lost, as long as they preserved their superior run rate. So, as *Wisden* put it: "The Somerset captain, Rose, sacrificed all known cricketing principles by deliberately losing the game."

After one over, with his team's score on 1 for 0, Rose shocked everyone by declaring. Worcestershire, with no chance to improve their run rate, bitterly knocked off the two runs they needed and the match was over in 20 minutes.

Rose's wheeze worked well – until Somerset were thrown out of the Cup for acting against the spirit of the game.

"We knew people weren't going to like us much, but the storm of controversy did take us by surprise. I regret it if we hurt the spirit of the game. Ironically it made us even more determined to win something." – BRIAN ROSE

ARJUNA RANATUNGA
'PUT ME THROUGH TO THE PRIME MINISTER!'

Much of Sri Lankan cricket's success in recent years can be attributed to their long-time skipper, Arjuna Ranatunga. The single-minded Ranatunga – nicknamed Napoleon – has frequently courted controversy, but never more so than in the triangular one-day tournament in Australia in 1999.

The action revolved (not for the first time) around star Sri Lankan spinner Muttiah Muralitharan and his 'unusual' bowling action. To avoid angst, the organisers had not matched the Sri Lankans with umpire Darrell Hair, who was known to rate Murali a chucker. But they had forgotten about Ross Emerson, who shared the same view as Hair – and in Sri Lanka's game against England he duly called Murali for throwing.

Ranatunga, incensed, led his players off the pitch in a protest that lasted 15 minutes. He was eventually persuaded to return, but not before he had apparently consulted the Sri Lankan government back home.

England captain Alec Stewart summed up Ranatunga's actions perfectly: "Your behaviour has been appalling for a country's captain."

'S RETREAT

Arjuna Ranatunga makes his point to Ross Emerson, who has just no-balled Muralitharan. Eventually, Ranatunga led his players off the field in protest (left)

DENNIS LILLEE
BAT-MAN

In his 14 years as a Test cricketer, Dennis Lillee was a constant thorn in England's side. Mainly this was through his bowling, which was always infuriatingly effective against the Poms. But during England's 1979/80 tour of Australia, in Perth the singleminded Lillee found a novel way of getting under the skin of the old enemy – as a batsman.

The moustachioed maestro took guard using a bat fashioned not from wood, but from aluminium. The prototype bat, in which Lillee had a proprietorial interest, immediately provoked a complaint from England skipper Mike Brearley and concern from the two umpires. Lillee was defiantly unmoved, however, and it took Aussie captain Greg Chappell, and ten heated minutes, to persuade Dennis the Menace to exchange it for the traditional willow.

Postscript – the aluminium bat was actually within the rules of the game, but the umpires, not surprisingly, ruled that it was outside the spirit.

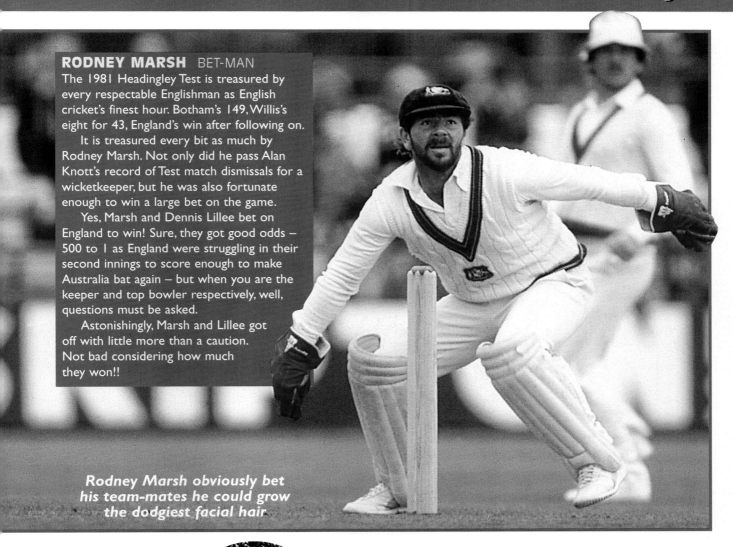

RODNEY MARSH BET-MAN

The 1981 Headingley Test is treasured by every respectable Englishman as English cricket's finest hour. Botham's 149, Willis's eight for 43, England's win after following on.

It is treasured every bit as much by Rodney Marsh. Not only did he pass Alan Knott's record of Test match dismissals for a wicketkeeper, but he was also fortunate enough to win a large bet on the game.

Yes, Marsh and Dennis Lillee bet on England to win! Sure, they got good odds – 500 to 1 as England were struggling in their second innings to score enough to make Australia bat again – but when you are the keeper and top bowler respectively, well, questions must be asked.

Astonishingly, Marsh and Lillee got off with little more than a caution. Not bad considering how much they won!!

Rodney Marsh obviously bet his team-mates he could grow the dodgiest facial hair

DERMOT REEVE
NO-BAT-MAN

Dermot Reeve has always been an original thinker – as cricketer, captain and, latterly, coach. One of his most interesting 'innovations' came in a match against Hampshire at the start of the 1996 season. Warwickshire were battling to avoid defeat in their second innings. Reeve, disconcerted by the turn and bounce generated by Raj Maru from the rough outside his leg stump, was worried about getting caught while playing defensively. Reeve's startling solution was to thrust his pad to the ball … and throw his bat away. He did this 15 times in his 89-ball innings.

He claimed it was within the rules of the game, but the MCC later ruled that the umpires could have 'seriously considered' giving him out for obstruction. Oh, and Warwickshire lost the match anyway.

DOUGLAS JARDINE
ENGLAND CAPTAIN AND WINNER!

The 1932/3 series in Australia is the most infamous in history. Three years earlier, England had been 'introduced' to Don Bradman, who had pulverised them in scoring 974 runs in the series. They needed some way to stop him, and England captain Douglas Jardine reckoned he had a solution.

With two very fast bowlers in his side – Harold Larwood and Bill Voce – and no restrictions on leg-side fielders, Jardine developed 'leg theory': fast, short-pitched balls aimed at the batsman's body. Even Bradman was unable to defend effectively against the tactic and England ran out 4-1 winners in the Ashes series.

Jardine was ruthless in his employment of the tactic, to the disgust of not only Australian players, but also Australian politicians – who nearly broke off diplomatic relations with Britain. Some of Jardine's own team were none too impressed either. The Nawab of Pataudi, for example, refused to join the leg-side field, leading to the immortal quote from Jardine: "His Excellency is a conscientious objector."

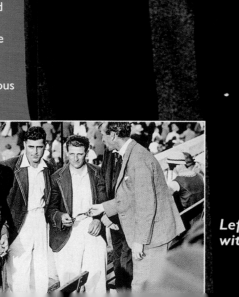

Left: Jardine (on right of picture) in 1932 with his henchmen, Larwood and Voce

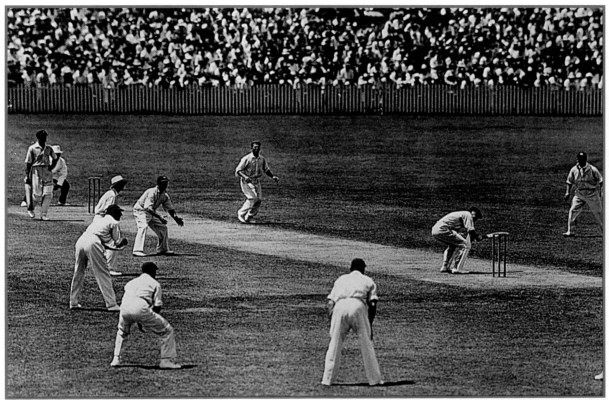

Australia captain Bill Woodfull ducks a Larwood bouncer during the Fourth Test at Brisbane. Bodyline had begun in earnest when Larwood hit Woodfull during the previous Test

WAR OF WORDS – WHAT THEY SAID ABOUT BODYLINE AT THE TIME

"Bodyline bowling has assumed such proportions as to menace the best interests of the game, making protection of the body by the batsmen the main consideration. This is causing intensely bitter feeling between the players as well as injury. In our opinion it is unsportsmanlike. Unless stopped at once, it is likely to upset the friendly relationships existing between Australia and England."
– *Text of the cable from the Australian Cricket Board to the MCC following the Adelaide Test, 1933*

"We, Marylebone Cricket Club, deplore your cable. We deprecate your opinion that there has been unsportsman-like play. We have fullest confidence in captain, team and managers and are convinced they would do nothing to infringe either the Laws of Cricket or the game."
– *Part of MCC's cabled reply, 1933*

"He can be a powerful friend but a relentless enemy. He gives no quarter and asks none. He is a fighter, every inch of him. He will see a job through, no matter what the consequences, and will never admit defeat."
– *Bill Bowes on Jardine, 1949*

"He is a queer fellow. When he sees a cricket ground with an Australian on it, he goes mad."
– *Sir Pelham Warner on Jardine, 1934*

TONY GREIG
GUN FOR HIRE

The game of cricket was rocked to its foundations in 1977 by World Series Cricket. In what was certainly the most significant cricket development in the 20th century, Kerry Packer, a media mogul of vast ego and equally vast pockets, drove a stake into the heart of the cricket establishment and changed the complexion of the game for ever.

The man at the centre of Packer's operation was Tony Greig. Greig had signed up as the principal recruiter for the Rest of the World team to take on the Australians, and began moving around like a secret agent, making approaches, persuading players, even setting up the deals. Yet he was also a current England international, and had actually been approached by Packer whilst captain in the Centenary Test.

By throwing in his lot with Packer, Greig became a pariah in English cricket, and less than two years after being captain of his country had ended his first-class career and emigrated to Australia. He was rarely seen here thereafter, being sighted only rarely and in the guise of "that twat who keeps sticking his car keys into the pitch".

Greig didn't have the bails to say no to Packer

AFTAB GUL
MISGUIDED MISSILE

Aftab Gul's career was dogged by political controversy. As a Pakistani student leader he enjoyed considerable power – so much so that in 1968 the student body threatened to disrupt a Test match against England if their man was not selected. The authorities gracefully caved in.

He won six caps and might have been remembered for his fine batting. But he continued to mix with politicos, and after a spell abroad was refused re-entry to Pakistan. The authorities claimed that a SAM-7 missile had been found under his bed and declared him persona non grata. Oh well, it's a new way of being told you're dropped.

BASIL D'OLIVEIRA
PREJUDICE-BUSTER

Things have changed a lot in South Africa in recent years. So much so that the official list of South Africa's top ten cricketers of the century featured a man who played 44 times for England and was instrumental in having his home country banned from international cricket for over 20 years. That man was Basil d'Oliveira.

Dolly had come to England from South Africa because his career was blocked in his home country on account of his skin colour. He played a few times for England and, although by no means a regular, it seemed that his 158 against Australia at The Oval in 1968 would cement his place in the team to tour South Africa that winter.

It was, however, known that South Africa's apartheid regime would object to the selection of a black man in the England team – and he was excluded (to widespread criticism) from the original party. But when Tom Cartwright dropped out, d'Oliveira was brought in as a replacement.

What followed is history. South African Prime Minister John Vorster refused to accept Dolly as a member of the MCC team, and the MCC promptly cancelled the tour.

Within a couple of years, South Africa were banned from Test cricket. D'Oliveira went on playing for England and, until Allan Lamb jumped ship, appeared in more Tests than the rest of the South Africans put together.

Basil d'Oliveira – the mild-mannered man at the eye of a political storm

...AND ELEVEN PLAYERS WHO'VE BEEN ACCUSED OF DUBIOUS PRACTICES

1 **MICHAEL ATHERTON**
Kept dirt in pocket 'to keep his hands dry', but was fined £2,000

2 **SHANE WARNE**
He and Mark Waugh admitted being paid by an Indian bookie for their 'opinions on the pitch'

3 **SALIM MALIK**
Shane Warne and Mark Waugh claimed he tried to bribe them;

4 **MUTTIAH MURALITHARAN**
Sri Lankan spinner no-balled for throwing – but only in Australia

5 **IAN MECKIFF**
Aussie no-balled for throwing – in Australia! – in 1963

6 **SHOAIB AKHTAR**
World's fastest bowler accused of throwing just when due to play Australia – there's a coincidence

7 **JOHN LEVER**
Accused of smearing ball with vaseline after 10-wicket debut in India in 1976/7, and was cleared

8 **ALF GOVER**
Cricket schools founder, accused of using hair oil on ball in '30s

9 **WASIM & WAQAR**
Constant insinuations about tampering with their balls

10 **SARFRAZ NAWAZ**
Sued Allan Lamb for claiming he'd admitted tampering; case withdrawn

11 **SALIM YOUSUF**
Never slow to claim a catch on the one hand one bounce rule

BIZARRE BOWLING LINE-UPS

In every generation there is a bowler who strikes fear into almost every batsman they face. It is not necessarily due to the fear of losing a wicket. It is the fear of being hit very hard in a place where it is likely to hurt – a lot. Some crazy batsmen claim that they enjoy facing fast bowlers. Not this fivesome…

The FEARSOME Fivesome

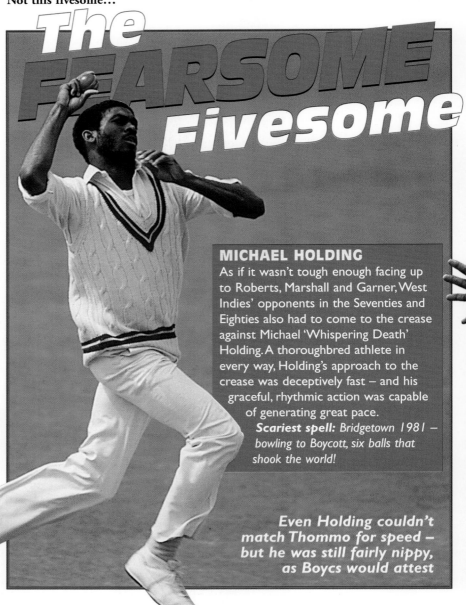

JEFF THOMSON

Jeff Thomson was a tearaway surf bum who burst on to the cricket scene with a bang in the early 1970s. With his unique slingshot action he was not always accurate, but he was always fast – the fastest ever, according to the speed gun. In a shootout between 12 top quicks in 1979, Thommo clocked 99.69mph – 12mph faster than the second best, Michael Holding. And, like the archetypal Aussie he was, he seemed to reserve his best for the old enemy, the Poms.

Scariest spell: MCG 1975 – removed first five West Indies wickets including Greenidge, Fredericks and Lloyd

> **'I enjoy hitting a batsman more than getting him out. I like to see blood on the pitch.'**
>
> JEFF THOMSON, 1974

MICHAEL HOLDING

As if it wasn't tough enough facing up to Roberts, Marshall and Garner, West Indies' opponents in the Seventies and Eighties also had to come to the crease against Michael 'Whispering Death' Holding. A thoroughbred athlete in every way, Holding's approach to the crease was deceptively fast – and his graceful, rhythmic action was capable of generating great pace.

Scariest spell: Bridgetown 1981 – bowling to Boycott, six balls that shook the world!

Even Holding couldn't match Thommo for speed – but he was still fairly nippy, as Boycs would attest

HAROLD LARWOOD

In most footage of cricket played in the black and white era, the game looks incredibly slow – particularly the bowlers who amble in off a five-stride run and deliver at gentle medium pace at best. Not so Harold Larwood, who manages to look quick and menacing whatever speed the film is playing at. Facing this man in 1933 must have seemed like a voyage into hell for the Aussies.

Scariest spell: First Test in Bodyline series at Sydney – must have come as a bit of a shock to those poor Aussies

"I used to give every new batsman four balls. One was a bouncer to check his courage, the second a fizzer to check his eyesight, the third a slow'un to try out his reflexes and the fourth a bender to see if he was a good cricketer. And if he took a single off each … I knew I was in trouble."
– HAROLD LARWOOD, 1972

SHOAIB AKHTAR

Was it any surprise that Shoaib Akhtar's action was called into question by the Australian-influenced ICC in early 2000? After all, the world's fastest bowler was due to face the Aussies in a one-day series, and we wouldn't want any of them to get hurt, would we? Can't blame them, though – they call him the Rawalpindi Express, and that's not because he keeps breaking down.

Scariest spell: World Cup 1999 vs Scotland at the Riverside – ripped through the Scots' upper order in ferocious fashion

MALCOLM MARSHALL

Fast bowlers in recent years have tended to look like rejects from the Harlem Globetrotters. Not so Malcolm Marshall, who was perhaps the most effective West Indian bowler of the pace era. Marshall was quick, but his main weapon was surprise. From his relatively short height, he was capable of bowling fearsome bouncers with no noticeable change in action. Just ask Mike Gatting.

Scariest spell: Sabina Park 1985 – destroyed Gatting's nose with a classic Marshall bouncer

BIZARRE BOWLING LINE-UPS

Cricket fans love a mystery bowler. The guy who bamboozles batsmen with his off spinners, leg spinners, flippers and – the classic favoured by most amateur spinners – the straight ball that keeps going straight. Sometimes he may have full control of his bowling; often he doesn't know what he's going to do until it's done. Because, like James Joyce's *Ulysses*, he's simply unreadable.

The UNREADABLES

SONNY RAMADHIN

Sonny Ramadhin arrived in England in 1950 having played only two first-class games (on matting) and with nothing known about him other than that he was a spin bowler from Trinidad who looked about 12 years old. By the time he had taken 11 wickets at Lord's, he was the talk of cricket. Bowling off breaks and leg breaks, he truly was a 'mystery' bowler. Later in his career he was found out by Cowdrey and May, but not before he had taken over 150 Test wickets.

B. J. T. BOSANQUET

Bernard Bosanquet, who played from 1898 to 1919, achieved fame on two counts. First, for being the father of the TV newsreader the late Reginald Bosanquet; and second, for developing the googly. Bosanquet, who was really a batsman, developed the ball – an off-break with a leg-break action – by playing billiards five or 'twisty grab'. No, we don't know what it is either, but we wouldn't want to play it without a box.

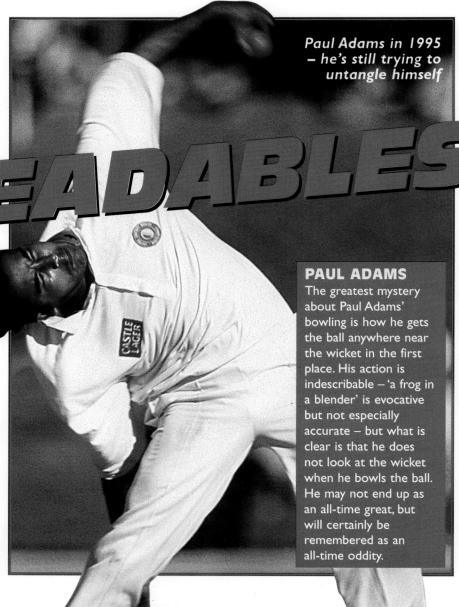

Paul Adams in 1995 – he's still trying to untangle himself

PAUL ADAMS

The greatest mystery about Paul Adams' bowling is how he gets the ball anywhere near the wicket in the first place. His action is indescribable – 'a frog in a blender' is evocative but not especially accurate – but what is clear is that he does not look at the wicket when he bowls the ball. He may not end up as an all-time great, but will certainly be remembered as an all-time oddity.

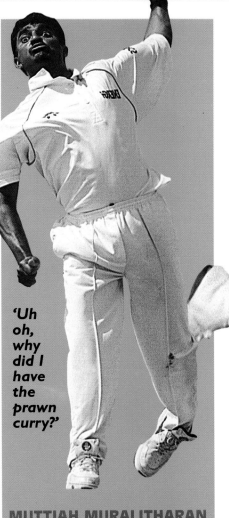

'Uh oh, why did I have the prawn curry?'

MUTTIAH MURALITHARAN

Whisper it softly: there's something decidedly odd about Murali's action … oh, you've heard. Muralitharan is not just unreadable – he's also unplayable and unpronounceable. He now seems to have developed a top spinner, which really isn't on for an off-spinner. It won't be long before the bounder bowls a leggie.

Changi… Chandri… Chandha… oh, that Indian guy in action

BHAGWAT CHANDRASEKHAR

For home Tests in India in the 1970s, seamers were normally considered an expensive luxury. India relied instead on spin – and with bowlers of the class of Bedi, Venkataraghavan and Chandrasekhar, this proved often to be a winning strategy. Of the three, Chandrasekhar was the most mysterious. Stricken by polio as a child, he developed his own unique style of leg spin and was capable of great variety. His only major disappointment was that, although he took more wickets than Venkat, his name still had fewer letters in it.

99

BIZARRE BOWLING LINE-UPS

Fast bowlers have always been emotional, aggressive buggers. Perhaps they have to be to bowl fast ball after ball after ball. Perhaps it's to cloak the pain they inflict on their bodies. Or perhaps they are simply mad. Most manage to contain their aggression to bowling and appealing, but once in a while things boil over. These are five of the best explosions of the pressure cooker.

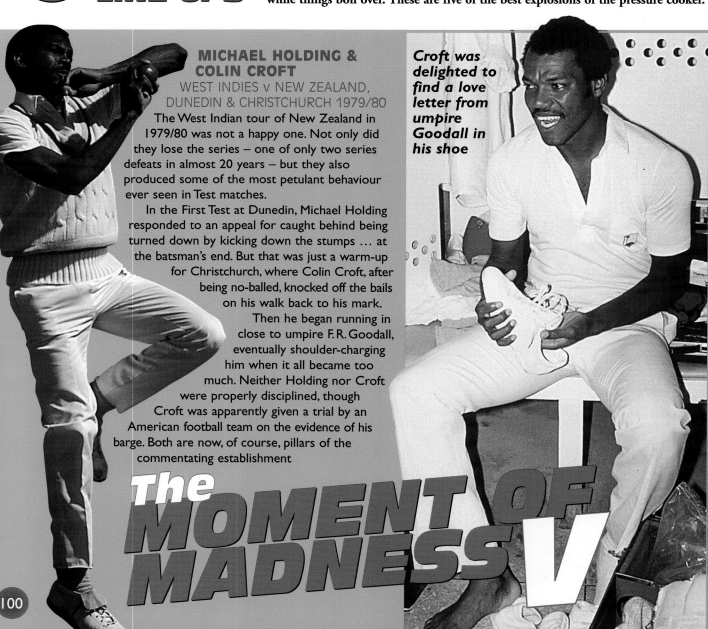

MICHAEL HOLDING & COLIN CROFT
WEST INDIES v NEW ZEALAND, DUNEDIN & CHRISTCHURCH 1979/80

The West Indian tour of New Zealand in 1979/80 was not a happy one. Not only did they lose the series — one of only two series defeats in almost 20 years — but they also produced some of the most petulant behaviour ever seen in Test matches.

In the First Test at Dunedin, Michael Holding responded to an appeal for caught behind being turned down by kicking down the stumps ... at the batsman's end. But that was just a warm-up for Christchurch, where Colin Croft, after being no-balled, knocked off the bails on his walk back to his mark.

Then he began running in close to umpire F. R. Goodall, eventually shoulder-charging him when it all became too much. Neither Holding nor Croft were properly disciplined, though Croft was apparently given a trial by an American football team on the evidence of his barge. Both are now, of course, pillars of the commentating establishment

Croft was delighted to find a love letter from umpire Goodall in his shoe

The MOMENT OF MADNESS V

SYLVESTER CLARKE
WEST INDIES v PAKISTAN, MULTAN 1980/81

Cricket crowds on the Indian sub-continent have always been a little volatile, and their standard of decorum has been known to leave something to be desired. In the Fourth Test at Multan, West Indian firebrand Sylvester Clarke was fielding on the boundary and getting a mite fed up with the barrage of oranges raining down on him from the terraces.

His reaction was probably not entirely advisable – to pick up a brick and throw it into the crowd.

In doing so he managed to knock out a student union president and cause a mini-riot in the stands. We believe he was moved to slip pretty soon after.

Wicked!

TERRY ALDERMAN
AUSTRALIA v ENGLAND, PERTH 1982

Most cricketers respond to pitch invasions with resigned amusement. Not so Terry Alderman. In the first Test of 1982, England actually passed 400 in their first innings – which was the signal for about 15 good honest English yeoman (yes, they were arseholed) to invade the pitch. One playfully cuffed Alderman about the head. Bad idea. Alderman gave chase and brought him down with a classic full-length rugby tackle. The tackle was good, the impact for Alderman's shoulder was not. Alderman dislocated it and had to sit out the rest of the season. It still didn't stop Australia winning the series. Bastards.

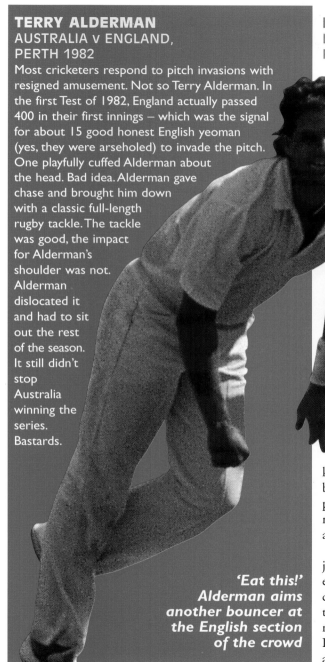

'Eat this!' Alderman aims another bouncer at the English section of the crowd

RASHID PATEL
DULEEP TROPHY FINAL, INDIA 1991

The reason usually cited by batsmen for wearing protective clothing is to avoid being injured by the ball. In the 1991 final of India's top tournament, the Duleep Trophy, opening bat Raman Lamba needed his to fend off an entirely different threat.

Lamba had managed to wind up West Zone bowler Rashid Patel to such an extent that Patel aimed a head-high beamer at Lamba. When this failed to knock the batsman's block off, Patel suddenly picked up a stump and ran down the wicket to attack Lamba.

Battle was then joined, bringing a swift end to the match and causing a serious riot in the crowd. History does not record whether Patel's weapon contained a stump camera.

BIZARRE BOWLING LINE-UPS

N ot all bowlers have their techniques and styles created out of the coaching manual. Many develop idiosyncratic styles that, whilst looking awful, can still be highly effective. We celebrate five of the best here, some clumsy, some quirky and some just … well, bizarre.

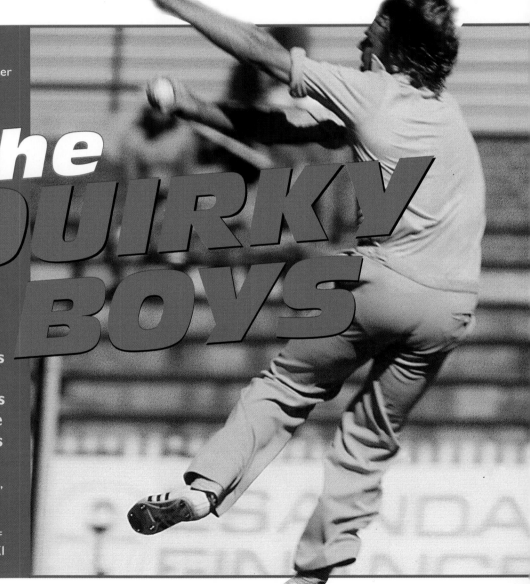

The QUIRKY BOYS

MIKE PROCTER

The massively gifted Mike Procter was a classical batsman, but anything but a classical bowler. Charging in to the wicket, he appeared to arrive on the wrong foot and to be rushed into bringing his arm over like a jet-powered windmill. Over 1,400 wickets would indicate that he was anything *but* clumsy, but who knows how many wickets he would have taken if he'd bowled correctly!

'When the force was with Mike Procter with the ball he was irresistible – and he was a most glorious batsman too.'

CHRISTOPHER MARTIN-JENKINS, EXPLAINING WHY HE WOULD CHOOSE THE SOUTH AFRICAN AS AN ALL-ROUNDER AHEAD OF IAN BOTHAM IN HIS WORLD XI

COLIN DREDGE

'Herbie' Dredge played for Somerset throughout their glory years from 1976 to 1988. About 6'8" tall, with a pronounced stoop and a loping gait, he was the most unlikely looking sportsman. His approach to the wicket was ponderous and his delivery ungainly. Though not quite as glamorous as team-mates Botham, Garner and Richards, the 'Demon of Frome' managed to take over 400 first class wickets and become a West Country folk hero.

Poetry in motion...

And what do you do?

Hate the Poms, ma'am

MAX WALKER

Never quite as celebrated as his strike partner Lillian Thomson, Max Walker was still good enough to take 138 wickets in Tests. Walker's nickname was Tangles – a fairly accurate comment on the mess he got himself into when delivering the ball. He bowled off the wrong foot, was totally open-chested, and seemed to bring his arm *through* his head rather than round its side. How he got it on target perhaps only he knows.

TONY GREIG

Tony Greig has largely been denied the respect his achievements deserve. Much was to do with his role in the Packer affair, but perhaps even more was the hilarious bowling style he developed late in his career. Looking like Basil Fawlty in his 'Don't mention the war' period – or the Minister for Silly Bowling Actions – and with massively exaggerated move-ment, he looked like he was taking the piss out of someone. Actually, he wasn't.

ASIF MASOOD

Once called Massif Arsood – possibly in error – by Brian Johnston, Asif Masood of Pakistan had perhaps the most eccentric action in the history of Test cricket. A medium fast bowler, Masood performed a backward sashay like a ballet dancer before starting his run-up. His approach to the wicket then compounded the comedy – "like Groucho Marx chasing a pretty waitress", as described by John Arlott.

BIZARRE BOWLING LINE-UPS

The days of the gentle "How's that?" are long gone – if they ever existed. But even now, when every bowler thinks every batsman got a nick to every wide, some guys are still more appealing than others…

PHIL TUFNELL
'Umpire! Umpire! I think I'm going to fart!'

RICHARD HADLEE
'Umpire! Umpire! I've farted too!'

FIVE DEMENTED APPEALERS

The BEST FOREIGNERS TO PLAY IN ENGLAND XI

'Look, Mum – clean undercrackers!'

In recent years debate has raged over whether it is good or bad for English cricket to have foreign imports in county sides. On the plus side they win lots of matches, finish top of the averages and generally show our players how to play. On the minus side they keep out of each county side one mediocre player. Mmm. Interesting argument.

What is indisputable is that, while some imports have been absolute disasters, the best have contributed handsomely to English county cricket. We pay tribute to some of those here.

Grandad shows off his cricket skills

THE BEST FOREIGNERS TO PLAY IN ENGLAND XI

1 Gordon Greenidge
2 Jimmy Cook
3 Phil Simmons
4 Asif Iqbal
5 Clive Rice
6 Mike Procter
7 Farokh Engineer
8 Richard Hadlee
9 Courtney Walsh
10 Franklyn Stephenson
11 Waqar Younis

GORDON GREENIDGE
HAMPSHIRE

Gordon Greenidge almost didn't make it into this XI … because he almost wasn't a foreigner. Brought to England from Barbados at the age of 12, and educated in Reading, Greenidge could have chosen his country of residence but instead chose his country of birth. The rest is history.

At county level he was a loyal servant of Hampshire, playing every season from 1970 to 1987 except when on tour with the Windies. He performed well for his county in all forms of cricket and at one time held the record for the highest score in each of the three one-day competitions.

Astonishingly, though, Hampshire – who for several seasons opened the batting with Greenidge and Barry Richards – never won a Lord's final with Greenidge in the side. They did, however, capture the Sunday League three times and Greenidge remains a legend in his adopted county.

'When Greenidge was in the mood there was no more devastating batsman in the game.'
— TONY COZIER

JIMMY COOK
SOMERSET

Jimmy Cook played three seasons only for Somerset and never saw them finish higher than 14th in the Championship, but in those three seasons he was unstoppable. In all matches for the county he scored 10,639 runs at 62.2, including 7,604 in first-class games at 72.4 including 28 hundreds. He was the highest runs-scorer in England in 1989 and 1991, and was edged out in 1990 only by Gooch in his golden summer. He made up for his disappointment in 1990, however, by scoring what was then a record 902 runs in the Sunday league.

Wisden recounted on his departure that he "never missed a match, was invariably lively in the field, always put the team's needs first and established a superb reputation for chivalry and modesty". Surely he couldn't have really been a South African?

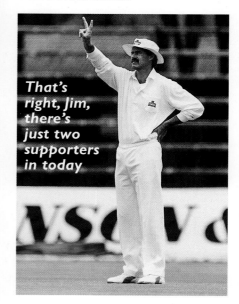

That's right, Jim, there's just two supporters in today

Phil always enjoyed his trips to Gower Manor

ASIF IQBAL
KENT

Asif Iqbal was a dynamic all-rounder who played 58 times for Pakistan and graced the Kent team from 1968 to 1982, captaining the side for two spells. An exciting batsman who could adapt to the needs of the moment, and an effective medium pace bowler, Iqbal played a big part in one of Kent's most successful periods. They won ten trophies during his time – three County Championships, three Sunday League titles, three B&H Cups and the Gillette Cup. Asif always gave his best and is fondly remembered by the Kent faithful.

PHIL SIMMONS LEICESTERSHIRE

Phil Simmons' introduction to first-class cricket in England was anything but auspicious. Going out to bat for the West Indian tourists at Bristol in fading light, he was struck on the head by a bouncer from David Lawrence and nearly killed. It was his first and only game of the tour. He recovered, but toured unsuccessfully in 1991 and played disappointingly for Leicestershire in 1994. When he returned in 1996 it was with a point to prove. Scoring more runs than any teammate *and* finishing top of their bowling averages, he was Leicestershire's key player in only their second ever Championship win. He then returned in 1998 to captain them to their third. A great team player, if not a great player, Simmons deserves the freedom of his county.

CLIVE RICE & RICHARD HADLEE
NOTTINGHAMSHIRE

From the Second World War right up till the late 1970s, Nottinghamshire were a very mediocre cricket side. Bottom of the Championship eight times and in the bottom five a further 12 times, they and their supporters were little used to success. All that changed with the arrival of Clive Rice from South Africa, followed by New Zealander Richard Hadlee.

At his peak, Rice was the best all-rounder in the world, ahead even of Botham. Hadlee was certainly the best bowler plying his trade in county cricket – while being no mean bat as well.

With Rice at the helm they drove Notts to Championship wins in 1981 and 1987. Yet they were no two-man team – the groundsman, Ron Allsopp, was almost as influential, producing 'sporting' pitches at Trent Bridge to suit the home attack – but Notts would not have won a bean without their twin titans, Rice and Hadlee.

Hadlee always bought his PJ's from Oxfam

TWIN PEAKS

MIKE PROCTER
GLOUCESTERSHIRE

South African all-rounder Mike Procter was so popular in his adopted Gloucestershire that many fans took to calling it Proctershire. The best batsman, bowler and fielder in the side for most of his 14 years there, he was able to dedicate himself to the county thanks to South Africa's exclusion from Test cricket.

He managed to power lightweight Gloucestershire to two one-day trophies in the Seventies and nearly helped them to their only Championship of the century. He had many fine moments, but is perhaps best remembered in this country for his four wickets in five balls – Greenidge, Richards, Jesty and Rice – in the 1977 B&H semi-final. On that day, he was simply too good.

FAROKH ENGINEER
LANCASHIRE

While there have been numerous batters and bowlers who have come to this country from overseas to display their talents, there have been few foreign keepers in the English game. It remains perhaps the only aspect of cricket – other than being good losers – in which we delude ourselves into thinking we still lead the world.

Perhaps the greatest wicketkeeping import was the dashing Farokh Engineer, who played for Lancashire from 1968 to 1976. Engineer was an ebullient, erratic player who was frequently brilliant, occasionally error-prone, but always entertaining. His time at Lancashire coincided with their emergence as a great one-day side, and he remains a popular figure with the fans to this day.

COURTNEY WALSH
GLOUCESTERSHIRE

After starting his career in an invincible West Indies side alongside the likes of Malcolm Marshall, Michael Holding and Joel Garner, Courtney Walsh has increasingly found himself in a side in which he is the only one who looks like taking a wicket. For Walsh this is not entirely a new experience, as he has carried the otherwise toothless Gloucestershire attack for most of the last 15 years. The fact that the Jamaican has kept going with no noticeable loss of commitment or effort is tribute to his innate will to win, his loyalty and his massive desire to take wickets.

Despite having one of the most comical batting styles in cricket, when it comes to bowling he simply does not know how not to give of his best. A true yeoman.

'If I was a bat maker I wouldn't want my logo on a bat used by Courtney.'
– GEOFFREY BOYCOTT

FRANKLYN STEPHENSON
NOTTINGHAMSHIRE/SUSSEX

Franklyn Stephenson remains the last player in England to perform the double of 1,000 runs and 100 wickets in a season, a feat he achieved in 1988 by scoring a hundred in each innings in the final match against Yorkshire. The man from Barbados had just stepped into the not inconsiderable boots of Richard Hadlee, and if anyone doubted him, he proved them wrong in some style.

Stephenson was top wicket-taker in each of his four seasons for Notts, then had four good seasons with Sussex. Although he led neither county to great success, he makes this XI on account of his legendary slower ball – a weapon so deadly it should have been legislated against.

WAQAR YOUNIS
SURREY/GLAMORGAN

It's hard to believe now, but in the 1970s and early 1980s Pakistan's 'pace' attack was about as potent as a 60-year-old man after a vasectomy. They had no genuinely quick bowlers and relied instead on spin and a little bit of, shall we say, ball management to take them to victory. How times have changed. We've had Shoaib, Aqib, Wasim and, of course, Waqar.

Never was a name more descriptive. Bowling extremely fast, Waqar Younis developed the inswinging yorker into an art form and was responsible for more broken toes than a concrete-kicking competition. For bringing this delivery to the UK and helping Glamorgan to a most unlikely Championship win in 1997, we include Waqar at number 11 in this side.

XI FOREIGNERS WHO DID NOT DISTINGUISH THEMSELVES

1. SHERWIN CAMPBELL *Durham 1996*
Campbell, now one of the Windies' most reliable batsmen, managed only one century for hapless Durham

2. RICHIE RICHARDSON *Yorkshire 1993-4*
In two seasons for the White Rose, averaged just over 30 before leaving halfway through season pleading exhaustion

3. DEAN JONES *Derbyshire 1996-7*
A fantastic success at Durham but walked out on Derbyshire after five games of the 1997 season

4. BRIAN LARA *Warwickshire 1996, 1998*
OK, so he played like a God – but he certainly wasn't the most popular guy in the dressing room

5. ADRIAN KUIPER *Derbyshire 1990*
South African middle order batsman, made the 12th-man position his own in disappointing season with Derbyshire

6. STEVE JEFFRIES *Hampshire 1988-9*
Left-arm swing bowler from South Africa who made more of an impact with the bat for Hants than with the ball – only 40 wickets in two seasons at 39 apiece

7. STEVE ELWORTHY *Lancashire 1996*
Didn't do himself justice in his one and only season at Lancs, averaging only 15 with the bat and over 40 with the ball

8. MOHAMMED AKRAM *Northamptonshire 1997*
Promising Pakistani seamer who fulfilled little of that promise as Northants finished fourth from bottom

9. DION NASH *Middlesex 1995-6*
After a decent debut season, returned in 1996 to play only one game before injury sent him home to New Zealand

10. DIRK TAZELAAR *Surrey 1989*
Queensland left-armer who took only seven wickets for 338 runs in his three games before returning home

11. CORRIE VAN ZYL *Glamorgan 1987-8*
Two sad seasons in South Wales for this South African fast bowler who took only 13 wickets at 56 apiece

... AND XI 'FOREIGNERS' WHO HAVE PLAYED FOR ENGLAND

1. **Paul Terry** Born Osnabruck, West Germany
2. **Mike Denness** Bellshill, Scotland
3. **Graeme Hick** Salisbury, Rhodesia
4. **Nasser Hussain** Madras, India
5. **Tony Greig** Queenstown, South Africa
6. **Adam Hollioake** Melbourne, Australia
7. **Dermot Reeve** Kowloon, Hong Kong
8. **Chris Lewis** Georgetown, Guyana
9. **Derek Pringle** Nairobi, Kenya
10. **Andy Caddick** Christchurch, NZ
11. **Devon Malcolm** Kingston, Jamaica

Nasser Hussain at home in Southend – or is it Madras? (Actually it's South Africa)

FIVE GREAT FIELDERS

The days when an overweight batsman could find a quiet haven in the outfield are long gone. Nowadays every fielder has to be able to sprint, dive, throw flat from the boundary and enthuse wildly throughout an entire day's toil. But if there are plenty of good fielders, there are still some who are exceptional. Here are five of the best.

JONTY RHODES

If cricketers were selected on fielding alone, Jonty Rhodes would be on every fantasy teamsheet for any team ever. He is quite simply brilliant in the field and lives up to the old adage that he starts each innings with 20 runs already on the board. A serious practising Christian, he shows little generosity when it comes to giving runs away and no mercy whatsoever about run-outs and catches. Great moments are many, but his pick-up, sprint and full-length dive to the stumps to run out Inzamam in the 1992 World Cup must rank as the greatest of them all.

GOTCHA!!

'It was pretty special. It won us the game.'
– KEPLER WESSELS ON JONTY RHODES' SPECTACULAR RUN-OUT OF INZAMAM IN THE 1992 WORLD CUP

*Clive Lloyd
mistakenly put
Hank Marvin
down at No.3*

VIV RICHARDS

The World Cup final of 1975 brought together the two powerhouses of Test cricket at the time, West Indies and Australia. The Windies included in their ranks a promising 23-year-old middle order batsman with but seven Tests to his name – Vivian Richards.

Richards, for once, failed with the bat. But he still managed to be the match-winner. Fielding at cover, he brilliantly ran out first Alan Turner, then Greg Chappell and finally captain Ian Chappell.

Lord's had never seen anything like it. The Master Blaster had arrived.

COLIN BLAND

Southern Rhodesia-born Colin Bland was a key player for South Africa in the 1960s, and was brilliant in all aspects of fielding. He was a superb catcher of the ball, could move like a panther in the covers, and his accuracy in hitting the stumps was unparalleled.

When the touring South Africans played at Canterbury in 1965, a wet wicket held up play and Kent captain Colin Cowdrey asked Bland if he would provide the restless crowd with an exhibition of fielding. A set of stumps was placed on the outfield and the ball was driven to Bland at various speeds and angles. From a distance of between 20 and 30 yards, he proceeded to flatten the stumps a phenomenal 12 times out of 15.

He did this time and again when it mattered, as well, and many observers judge him to be the greatest of all time.

LEARIE CONSTANTINE

Learie (later Lord) Constantine was one of the most dynamic cricketers the game has ever seen. The West Indian's batting was unorthodox and explosive – and his bowling fast and aggressive.

But it was his fielding that really distinguished him. He was superb in every position on the field. In the covers he was omnipresent and indeed omnipotent; in the deep he was one of the first players to pick up and throw in one movement at pace; and up close he was fearless with great reactions.

A pioneer for race relations as well as for cricket in the 1920s and '30s, he delighted fans wherever he played.

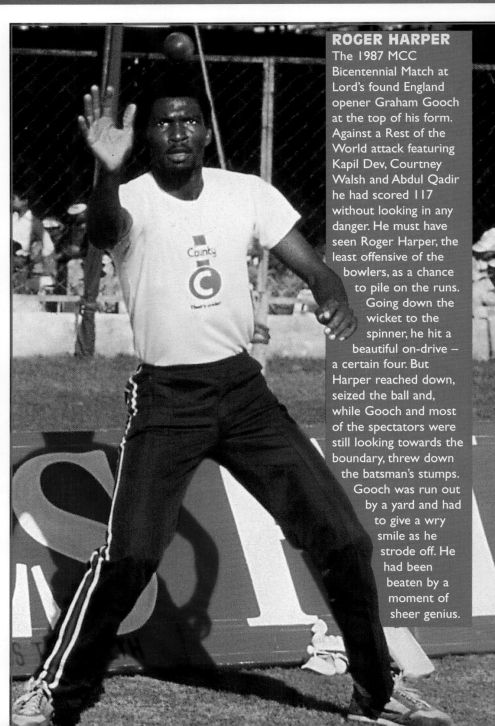

ROGER HARPER

The 1987 MCC Bicentennial Match at Lord's found England opener Graham Gooch at the top of his form. Against a Rest of the World attack featuring Kapil Dev, Courtney Walsh and Abdul Qadir he had scored 117 without looking in any danger. He must have seen Roger Harper, the least offensive of the bowlers, as a chance to pile on the runs. Going down the wicket to the spinner, he hit a beautiful on-drive – a certain four. But Harper reached down, seized the ball and, while Gooch and most of the spectators were still looking towards the boundary, threw down the batsman's stumps. Gooch was run out by a yard and had to give a wry smile as he strode off. He had been beaten by a moment of sheer genius.

... AND FIVE FAMOUS FIELDING ERRORS

B.A.BARNETT
1938 AUSTRALIA v ENGLAND

In 1938, Aussie keeper B. A. Barnett missed a simple stumping off the bowling of L. O'B. Fleetwood-Smith that would have dismissed Len Hutton. Hutton, who had scored 40 at that point, went on to make a record 364, while Fleetwood-Smith finished with the embarrassing figures of one for 298. Barnett never played another Test.

DON TOPLEY
1984 ENGLAND v WEST INDIES

Don Topley of Essex achieved early cricketing fame in 1984 while still a lad on the Lord's groundstaff. Brought on as a sub in the Test, he took an amazing one-handed catch on the boundary to dismiss Malcolm

Marshall. Well, he would have dismissed him ... if his back foot had not been over the rope as he took the catch. Result, one six and one nearly great moment for Topley to tell the grandkids about.

ROGER DAVIS
1968 GLAMORGAN v NOTTINGHAMSHIRE

Poor old Malcolm Nash is known for little else in his career other than being the bowler whom Gary Sobers hit for six sixes in one over. It could all have been so different. Off his fifth ball, Roger Davis managed to grasp the flying bullet right on the boundary rope. Unfortunately for Nash – and fortunately for Sobers – Davis fell backwards in the attempt and over the rope, and a six was given. The rest is cricket history.

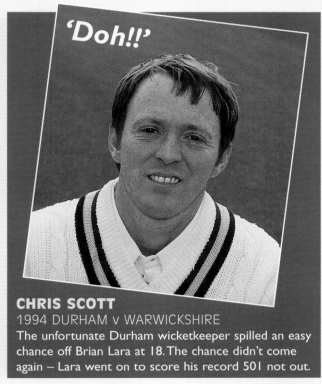

'Doh!!'

HERSCHELLE GIBBS
1999 WORLD CUP SOUTH AFRICA v AUSTRALIA

Gibbs' premature celebration of a catch off Steve Waugh led to him dropping the ball. Waugh went to score 120 not out and Australia won by one run, condemning the Springboks to meet (and lose to) their nemesis again in the semi-finals

'Doh!!'

CHRIS SCOTT
1994 DURHAM v WARWICKSHIRE

The unfortunate Durham wicketkeeper spilled an easy chance off Brian Lara at 18. The chance didn't come again – Lara went on to score his record 501 not out.

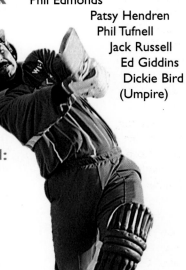

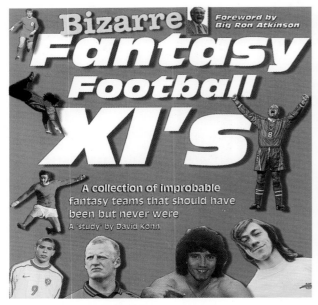

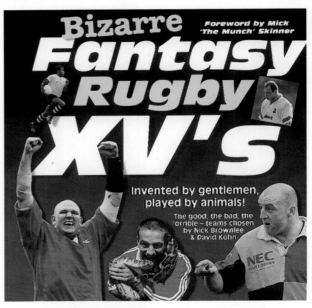

BIZARRE FANTASY FOOTBALL XI'S

BIZARRE FANTASY RUGBY XV'S

Indulge your fantasies...

THE 100 GREATEST CRICKETERS

THE 100 GREATEST MOMENTS IN CRICKET

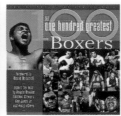

THE 100 GREATEST BOXERS

THE 100 GREATEST FOOTBALLERS

THE 100 GREATEST MOMENTS IN FOOTBALL

OFFSIDE

SECONDS OUT

ONLY FOOLS & HORSES

POWER FAILURE

FORMULA ONE MAD

All these books are available in bookshops, or can be ordered direct from: Generation Publications, 9 Holyrood St, London SE1 2EL. Please list the titles you want, with your name and address. Send a cheque or PO for £7.99 for each book plus £1 P&P for the first book, 50p for the second, and 30p for each additional book. (Overseas please double the P&P.)